# Social Enterprise in China

This book explores social innovation and entrepreneurship in China. Focusing on selected social enterprises and processes, it addresses the question of "where to, China?," not in terms of military, economic, or political ambitions, but in the terms of social innovation and welfare policies. The analyses range from detailed ethnography to discussions of broad global trends.

Despite vastly improved social conditions in the country, there are still unresolved issues that social enterprises address. The study elaborates on the complexities involved in their positioning between the state and their beneficiaries. Adding to the complexity is China's dual system of circulation and the moral economy of ethnic minorities. The theoretical foundation of the study is the Durkheimian concept of the social contract. Its content is viewed as comprised of Maussian total social facts or *guanxi*, a similar Chinese framing, operationalised to particular sociocultural configurations. The empirical cases document how social enterprises reposition elements in the various configurations in order to mobilise resources from their stakeholders. The book concludes that the discursive topology is altered in the process and the social contract is renewed in culturally meaningful, if paradoxical, ways.

This book will be of interest to researchers, students, and academics in the fields of business and social entrepreneurship, especially to those with a particular interest in the Chinese case.

**Benedicte Brøgger** is professor in the Department of Communication and Culture at the BI Norwegian Business School, Norway.

## Routledge Studies in Management, Organizations and Society

This series presents innovative work grounded in new realities, addressing issues crucial to an understanding of the contemporary world. This is the world of organized societies, where boundaries between formal and informal, public and private, local and global organizations have been displaced or have vanished, along with other 19th-century dichotomies and oppositions. Management, apart from becoming a specialised profession for a growing number of people, is an everyday activity for most members of modern societies.

Similarly, at the level of enquiry, culture and technology, and literature and economics, can no longer be conceived as isolated intellectual fields; conventional canons and established mainstreams are contested. *Management, Organizations and Society* addresses these contemporary dynamics of transformation in a manner that transcends disciplinary boundaries, with books that will appeal to researchers, students, and practitioners alike.

Recent titles in this series include:

**Industry 4.0**
A Glocal Perspective
*Edited by Jerzy Duda and Aleksandra Gąsior*

**Pierre Bourdieu in Studies of Organization and Management**
Societal Change and Transforming Fields
*Edited by Sarah Robinson, Jette Ernst, Kristian Larsen, and Ole Jacob Thomassen*

**Self-Management, Entrepreneurial Culture, and Economy 4.0**
A Contemporary Approach to Organizational Theory Development
*Edited by Agnieszka Rzepka, Zbigniew Olesiński, and Elżbieta Jędrych*

**Social Enterprise in China**
*Benedicte Brøgger*

# Social Enterprise in China

Benedicte Brøgger

LONDON AND NEW YORK

First published 2022
by Routledge
2 Park Square, Milton Park, Abingdon, Oxon OX14 4RN

and by Routledge
605 Third Avenue, New York, NY 10158

*Routledge is an imprint of the Taylor & Francis Group, an informa business*



*British Library Cataloguing-in-Publication Data*
A catalogue record for this book is available from the British Library

*Library of Congress Cataloguing-in-Publication Data*
Names: Brøgger, Benedicte, author.
Title: Social enterprise in China / Benedicte Brøgger.
Description: 1 Edition. | New York, NY : Routledge, 2022. |
Series: Routledge studies in management, organizations and society |
Includes bibliographical references and index.
Identifiers: LCCN 2021023128 (print) | LCCN 2021023129 (ebook) |
ISBN 9780367244613 (hardback) | ISBN 9781032128313
(paperback) | ISBN 9780429282591 (ebook)
Subjects: LCSH: Social entrepreneurship--China. | Social contract. |
Social change--China.
Classification: LCC HD60.5.C5 B76 2022 (print) | LCC HD60.5.C5
(ebook) | DDC 338/.040951--dc23
LC record available at https://lccn.loc.gov/2021023128
LC ebook record available at https://lccn.loc.gov/2021023129

ISBN: 978-0-367-24461-3 (hbk)
ISBN: 978-1-032-12831-3 (pbk)
ISBN: 978-0-429-28259-1 (ebk)

DOI: 10.4324/9780429282591

Typeset in Sabon
by MPS Limited, Dehradun

# Contents

# Lists of Illustrations

## Figures



## Tables

# Abbreviations

| | |
|---|---|
| ACFIC | All China Federation of Industry and Commerce |
| ASEAN | Association of South-East Asian Nations |
| CCP | Chinese Communist Party |
| CDPF | China Disabled Persons' Federation |
| EU | European Union |
| FBO | Faith-based organisation |
| GONGO | Government-organized non-governmental organization |
| HDI | Human Development Index |
| MLP | National Medium and Long-term Plan for Science and Technology Development |
| NCCCP | National Congress of the Chinese Communist Party |
| NGO | Non-governmental organization |
| NIS | National innovation system |
| NPC | The National People's Congress of the People's Republic of China |
| PRC | People's Republic of China |
| RNGO | Religious non-governmental organisation |
| SEZ | Special Economic Zone |
| SOE | State owned enterprise |
| TVE | Township and village enterprise |
| UN | United Nations |
| UNDP | United Nations Development Program |

# Preface

This book is written for people who are interested in social change in China, whether for academic or practical reasons. Disruptive technological innovations, economic growth, and radical political changes have visibly transformed the country. Even so, what will make the difference in the end, is how the social relations are changed. Here there is much to learn from the country's social enterprises and their gentle, considerate changemaking.

The idea for a book about social enterprises in China grew out of my experiences while I was working in Shanghai in 2017. Between teaching and administrative duties, I was writing up my research in a book on social entrepreneurship in Norway. Naturally, I became interested in local social entrepreneurs and enterprises and the particulars of doing business in this manner in China.

# Acknowledgements

In business studies, enterprises are focal points, much as stars are in astronomy. Astronomers investigate the unknown dark matter, which makes up most of the universe. They ask why some stars shine steadily, while others light up and go out. Business researchers think about enterprises in much the same terms but, unlike stars, businesses have to make a profit to keep running. What conditions success? What is in the dark matter, or "black boxes" as we call them? Answers have been found at the micro-level of the individual, the meso-level of the enterprise, and at the aggregate level of macroeconomics, geopolitics, and statistics.

I am as fascinated by enterprises as any business scholar but I am also a trained social anthropologist. In my research, I invariably home in on what is between people, the quality, and the order of relations. When a new phenomenon, social enterprises, appeared on the research horizon in the early 2000s, I was intrigued. Businesses that did not aim for profit? Businesses started to make a social impact? Private venture capital investing in community development, and expecting a return? For years, I grappled with the new phenomenon, along with other researchers and social entrepreneurs. Without the many explorations and conversations with them, this book would not have been possible.

The Entrepreneurship community of the European Academy of Management (EURAM) is a key arena for new knowledge. The papers I have read and presented at the *Social entrepreneurship and societal change* standing track has been an invaluable source of comparative insight as have the many discussions about how to conceptualise social entrepreneurship with Lucrezia Songini, Marzena Starnawska, Massimiliano Pellegrini, and Mathias Raith.

My fellow anthropologists Inga Treitler, Lotta Bjørklund Larsen, Tone Danielsen, Carla Dahl-Jørgensen, and Ralph Bolton have offered constructive critique to my writings and ideas over many years. Through them, I have managed to hook up with the tiny cluster of anthropologists interested in business at the Norwegian Anthropological Association (NAF), the European Association of Social Anthropologists (EASA), and the American Association of Anthropology (AAA). Our attempts to launch organisational anthropology, business anthropology, or fiscal anthropology have not caught on, but they sure have been inspiring.

Discussions with colleagues and students at the Fudan School of Management during my Shanghai stay provided invaluable insight into the thinking about market reforms in China. As my supporter while I was a visiting scholar, the Nordic Centre at the University of Fudan was a home during my stay. The unassuming and inclusive manner of the Centre's director Magnus Jorem provided a safe atmosphere for remarkably fun and open dialogues with other visiting scholars and local academics.

My wonderful colleagues in the Department of Culture and Communication at BI Norwegian Business School contributed with their numerous critical questions about the arguments of the book at our research seminars. Special thanks to Sut I Wong, Kristian Alm, and Anne Britt Gran for their input about China, ethics, and generalisations. Thanks to BI for financial support for travel and research assistance. Synonym's Helen Karlsen has done wonders to the text with her tactful nudging towards a proper English.

As always, thanks to my husband Bjørn and our children, Therese, Susanne, Andreas, and Thomas, their spouses and children, for their unwavering support.

# Understanding Chinese Business Practices

My interest in Chinese business practices started in the early 1980s. For my degree, I wanted to do longitudinal anthropological fieldwork in southern China to learn how market mechanisms were implemented in practice. As it was next to impossible to get the necessary research permits, I turned to the emerging Asian economic "tiger," Malaysia. That economic miracle was every way as intriguing as the reforms in China. Overseas Chinese entrepreneurs were a driving force in the Malaysian economy. I moved to Penang, where ethnic Chinese made up the majority of the population. An honorary secretary general of the Khoo kongsi, one of the richest and most influential lineage associations in South-East Asia, the late George Khoo took me under his wing. He taught me Chinese traditions and brought me to meet with other influential figures, among them former Capitan Cinas, who represented Chinese communities in colonial times. The Mahjong and excursions with a group of retirees were fun and relaxing, but I was too intent on gaining access to the business community to appreciate their wealth of knowledge about the workings of Chinese society in general.

In the 1990s, doing research for my Ph.D. I was fortunate enough to study the world of the kongsis. This time in Singapore. According to modernisation theory, this type of old-fashioned institution is bound to disappear. However, in Singapore, new ones were regularly being registered. My theory was that it was due to their position in civil society as repositories of cultural traditions, needed in a multi-ethnic city-state grappling with its identity. I was quite wrong. The reason was the opening up of China. Foreign Direct Investment from overseas Chinese was the most important source of foreign capital in China in those years. Investors were very welcome. The overseas Chinese investors had the opportunity to go back to the ancestral villages that figured so prominently in rituals and ceremonies. The price they had to pay was to invest in a factory, support a school, hospital, or build a road. This was no problem. Building institutional infrastructure had been the role of the kongsis in colonial time, anyway, as the British provided little in terms of social services.

The kongsi connections brought me to southern China in 1997. On a drive along the coast, kongsi name after kongsi name appeared on the road signs. Seeing the organisations materialise in this way was an eerie experience. Their names had been neat placeholders for information on my huge organisation chart of the 300 or so associations in Singapore. Now they became places, real in time and space. I saw a sign to the ancestral home of another of my mentors. Locally he was a war hero, but he had fought in the jungles against the communists in the 1950s Malayan uprising and had not had the chance to visit. He had kept up his filial duties in the kongsi instead. Now I was here, where he should have been.

After a long drive, our host stopped the car at a look-out point. The sea was visible just behind a street where long rows of houses were being built. The ground level shops were open for business. In the two or three floors above them, people had obviously moved in because there were clothes hanging out to dry and plants on the windowsills. Above, new floors were under construction. I was struck by the energy as I watched the teeming life, and the buildings visibly rising. Our host proudly talked about the economic boom in the area. He was born in the mid 1950s into a prominent Party family. Looking at the hope and trust expressed by the houses and reflecting on the famines, purges and reforms that had happened in his lifetime, I had to ask, "How can you go on?" He looked at me for a while and answered simply, "How can we not?"

Indeed, how can we not? All of us have to manage in the conditions we find ourselves in. Most of us manage to make a living and deal with our own everyday concerns as best we can. The social enterprises, however, go the extra mile in dealing with the everyday concerns of others. Too numerous to name individually, each and every one of the social entrepreneurs I met in China has shown what a difference social enterprises make, in the lives of the founders as much as of the beneficiaries. I wish all of you, who would embark on such a worthy venture, success with your ventures.

# Introduction

## Introduction

"It's complicated," said a young unemployed writer when I asked him how the Chinese Communist Party (CCP) engaged with social enterprises in China. He had given me a recent report on social enterprises in the country (Zhou et al., 2013) and wanted to discuss it as he was considering starting one himself. Despite my every effort, he did not answer my question but "deflected and defused" as I saw it. About a year later, when I asked the fundraising manager of a successful social enterprise how they could refuse government requests after having been granted free land for their building, she laughed, saying, "We find a way to say no." At first I interpreted statements like "it's complicated" and "ways to say no" as having to do with political control. It turned out to be far more complex than that, especially in discussions about social enterprises.

The aim of this book is to dig into China's emergent (post-)modern social discourse by exploring this complexity. After 30 years of communist rule, followed by 40 years of gradual market reform, there are predictions that strengthened authoritarianism will undermine China's stability and growth (Minzner, 2019). Which collectivities/communities will provide social glue in this new situation? I will discuss this and related issues in the light of Durkheimian perspectives that relations between state and society rest on a largely implicit social contract. My claim is that instead of deteriorating into dictatorship or predatory competition, the social forces in China are creating a new, distinct and distinctly different Chinese society.

The Chinese are engaged in statecraft, which is a defining characteristic of Chinese political life (Bøckmann, 2008, p. 40), but in the new situation, grassroots and businesspeople, who have traditionally been of low social status, are being mobilised too. Now many take social responsibility in a myriad of small ways that mainly go under the radar of the elite and produce a meaningful story and criteria for assessing truth (in the narrow sense of experiential social reality). Using social enterprises as cases, I show how vested interests engage outside the formal institutions and discuss their impact in terms that are neither communist nor capitalist. Most social

DOI: 10.4324/9780429282591-101

enterprises in China are registered as non-profit associations but are engaged in business-like activities to finance their operations. I therefore use the term "social enterprise" as a gloss for a variety of organisational types engaged in social work or social and cultural sustainability, but not formally part of the government's education, culture, community, or health and social services.

The National Congress of the Chinese Communist Party (NCCCP) and the National People's Congress of China (NPC), the supreme governing bodies of China, have both been drawing up comprehensive social innovation policies and legislation, setting up a number of political bodies, and funding research and education to reduce poverty and illiteracy. The starting up of social enterprises is part of this process. National policies certainly shape the social start-ups, but their connections to the global social enterprise movement are equally important. Chinese social enterprise start-ups are poised between the conflicting influences of global pro-democracy, pro-market, and pro-human rights forces and the dominant Marxist-Leninist-Maoist ideology of the CCP-controlled Chinese government.

## A global social enterprise movement

The global movement has come together from many sources and has paved the way for a Chinese social enterprise movement (Zhang, 2017). Many participants in the movement aim to create a new economic order, a viable alternative to global capitalism. While that has not happened, the alternative economic thinking has brought changes to how economies are set up and run, which is no small feat in itself.

Many countries are developing legal, financial, and institutional infrastructures that support social enterprises and new social industries are emerging. There are few national or international laws and regulations in this regard, but numerous international certification and assessment bodies exist. Even so, there are no reliable figures about the number of social enterprises globally. National statistics bureaux have problems getting the numbers right as only some countries have applicable legal company forms and there is no generally accepted definition of a social enterprise, at least not yet.

Broadly, a social enterprise can be defined as a non-government owned unit with a social mission. An iconic example is the Greyston Bakery in New York (http://greystonbakery.com). This social enterprise does not employ people to make cookies, but makes cookies to employ people (Ellis, 2010). Rough estimates from a few countries provide an indication of the number of social enterprises in these countries. However, there does not seem to be any pattern in the number of enterprises, the number of people, and social needs. A comparison of five countries, each with an especially relevant feature, highlights this point (see Table 0.1). India, known for its

*Table 0.1* Number of social enterprises in different countries

| *Country* | *Population (million), 2020* | *HDI rank, 2020* | *Estimated number of social enterprises, broad definition* | *Estimated number of social enterprises, narrow definition* | *Source* |
|---|---|---|---|---|---|
| India | 1380 | 131 | 2 000 000 | n.a. | British Council 2017. Note 2 |
| Kenya | 143 | 53 | 40 000 | n.a. | British Council 2017. Note 3 |
| Russia | 147 | 52 | 50 000 | n.a. | Tass, 2020. Note 4 |
| Brazil | 212 | 84 | 20 000 | n.a. | Letelier, 2012. Note 5 |
| Belgium | 11.5 | 13 | 19 000 | n.a. | Huybrechts et al., 2016 |
| Norway | 5.5 | 1 | n.a. | 234 | Kobro, 2019. Note 6 |
| China | 1,400 | 85 | n.a. | 295 | Yu, 2020. |

innovative social sector, is ranked number 131 on the Human Development Index (HDI),[1] has a population of about 1.380 billion and about two million social enterprises.[2] Kenya, the first country in the world to establish a social stock exchange, ranks 143 on the HDI, has 53 million inhabitants and around 40,000 social enterprises.[3] Russia, with its long collaborative tradition, ranks 52, has a population of 147 million and about 50,000 social enterprises.[4] Brazil, known for its long history of social cooperatives, ranks number 84, has 212 million people and an estimated 20,000 social enterprises.[5] Belgium, with the world's best developed legal infrastructure for social entrepreneurship is ranked number 13, has a population of 11.5 million and about 19,000 social enterprises (Huybrechts et al., 2016).

Based on a narrow definition of social enterprises, the numbers are much smaller. According to a European Commission definition, a social enterprise uses its surpluses mainly to achieve social goals; is managed in an accountable, transparent and innovative way and involves all stakeholders.[6] Based on this definition, there are 295 social enterprises in Norway, which ranks first on the HDI and has about five million inhabitants. In China, based on a similar precise definition, the number is 234 (Yu, 2020). China ranks 85 on the HDI and has a population of 1.4 billion. As these numbers illustrate, there is no apparent connection between the number of social enterprises, level of development, number of inhabitants, social enterprise infrastructure or collaborative traditions. The lack of agreement about definitions demonstrates that social entrepreneurship is an emergent academic discourse with theories and research methods still being tested (Nicholls, 2012).

The discussion about what social enterprises are and what they do is even more charged outside academia. Once a manager from a large telecommunication corporation spoke up during a seminar where I gave a talk about social enterprises in Norway. He said that the distinction between social and commercial was useless. His company made it possible for people to communicate, so had social impact and therefore was a social enterprise. Despite counterarguments from the audience and me, he refused to think differently.

What *is* certain though, is the social reality of the global social enterprise movement. That became abundantly clear in 2012 when Salesforce Inc. tried to trademark the term "social enterprise." Salesforce is a US-based unicorn, a technology start-up worth 1 billion USD or more. Its business idea is a cloud-based customer relation management (CRM) system. The news that Salesforce tried to claim ownership of the term spread like wildfire and caused a global digital outrage. Usually a disorganised mass of people and activities, in this instance the community coalesced into a collective force. For weeks, both the company and social media were bombarded with written protests, ranging from pleas to respect the digital commons to threats that Salesforce would be sued for theft. Salesforce lost credibility in the digital community and decided to reframe their new line of business.[7] This assertive global movement had a decisive influence on social enterprises in China, especially when they first appeared in the early 2000s. After this they slowly carved out space in the political economy, becoming distinctly *Chinese* social enterprises in the process.

## The setting

China offers very different conditions for social enterprises depending on location. Although geography is not a major topic in this book, it does play a role, and hence a brief overview of the country is in order.

China is more like a continent than a country. It is the third largest country in the world in terms of area, and borders on 14 other countries. The population was 1.4 billion in 2020. The majority live in densely populated industrialised areas along the coast and in the fertile agricultural areas in central China. In addition, there are enormous, almost unpopulated mountain ranges and deserts to the west. China has the largest number of megacities in the world. Depending on the definition, they number between 10 and 20. Even so, the majority of people live in villages and smaller townships. The social issues in the urban and rural areas are different, as are the means of addressing them.

The dominant ethnic group is Han Chinese, a range of people with similar languages and customs. In addition, there are 55 officially recognised minority ethnic groups. The ethnic minorities have social issues of their own to deal with. Some live peacefully with the majority, others are discriminated against and exploited. The majority of the country's ethnic minorities live in the remote western regions.

China has a planned economy, with centrally determined general goals and quotas and state-owned enterprises dominating all industries deemed strategically important. The economy is labour-intensive and reliant on natural resources, both domestic and imported. It is also being rapidly digitalised. The political system is authoritarian. China is a de facto one-party state dominated by the CCP. The eight other legal parties organise stakeholder interests and function as sounding boards for deliberation.

China has 31 provinces, further subdivided into prefectures, municipalities, counties, and townships. Economic and political conditions vary greatly between provinces, as do material and immaterial life quality. So, instead of regarding China as a country, in terms of the needs that social enterprises aim to meet, it is more realistic to think of it as a vast, diverse continent.

## The social contract

Durkheim's theory of the social contract holds that all contracts depend on conditions outside of the affairs regulated by the contract itself (Durkheim, 2018). Such conditions are customs, routines, morality, all of which constitute social reality and are not legally codified. Knowledge of these conditions is gained and transferred through practical experience or the kind of empirical research that Durkheim pioneered. Its empirical material is cultural rules or institutional structures that are external to individuals, what he called social facts. By researching social facts, it was possible to identify the order in a seemingly unregulated society. Durkheim studied society both in the sense of private life and civil society (the world of professional organisations, religious bodies and independent bureaux). He theorised that society exists *sui generis* and is qualitatively different from the worlds of politics and the economy. His theory opened up for the understanding of society as a distinct phenomenon. The goings-on could not be reduced to either political manoeuvring or economic dispositions.

The Durkheimian conception of the social contract led to more nuanced perspectives on the transactions between state and (civil) society, regulated by the social contract (see Figure 0.1. below). Interaction is not regulated merely by laws issued by the state, but also according to customary ways of doing things, unspoken norms, etiquette, and accepted social distinctions between groups of people. Durkheim was concerned with what he called "anomie," the breakdown of established moral standards in 1800s France in the midst of a transformation from an agrarian to an industrial economy. In particular, he was concerned with the moral position of the state. His theory is no less valid for understanding China in the midst of a transformation from an industrial to a digital economy. Three characteristics of the regulatory regime deserve special attention. One is that China is

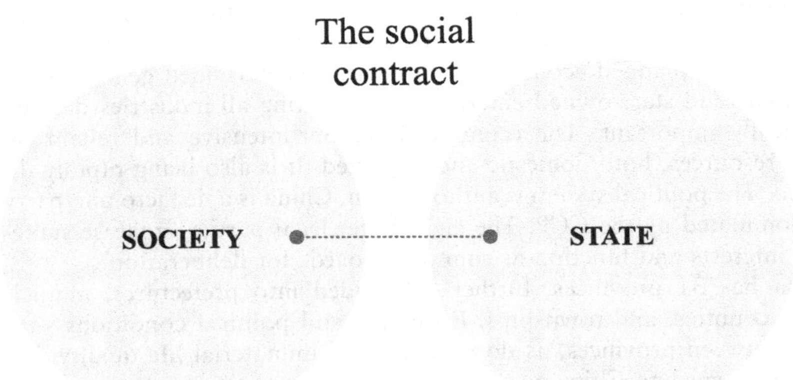
The social contract
SOCIETY
STATE
The social enterprises are changing the social contract in China

*Figure 0.1* A Durkheimian approach.

a one-party state with a planned economy. The government includes both the (relatively) independent civil service and the controlling CCP. Another condition is that there is no civil society in the Western sense of an independent public sphere. However, there are a range of, if not independent bodies, then certainly unruly ones, with which the government must contend (Gåsemyr, 2017; Pan, 2017). The third condition is the law itself, which includes not only formal laws, regulations, and rulings, but also communiques, campaigns and pledges made by officials (O'Brien & Li, 2006). The regulatory regime conditions the social contract.

The social contract, however, is not static but shaped by a particular form of statecraft. The original definition of statecraft is, in the narrow sense, of political leaders gaining control by "winning elections and achieving some necessary degree of governing competence in office" (Bulpitt, 1986, p. 21). However, "the formidable tradition of Chinese statecraft is much more sophisticated than just control mechanisms" (Bøckmann, 2008, p. 40). In this broader sense, statecraft also includes the means to assure broad political commitment. In the more dialectic understanding of statecraft used here, statecraft in China refers to the force of the government in all aspects of life in China, be it high-level political events or mundane everyday activities, *and* the counterforce of the myriad actions, political and economic, from wider Chinese society. One example is rightful resistance, the not-quite-political political actions that Chinese people organise to change government decisions (O'Brien & Li, 2006). Another is the interplay between ideological and economic considerations within many

Chinese companies (Li & Soobaroyen, 2021). In line with this broader understanding, I use "statecraft" as a gloss for the innovative ways that conflicting institutional demands are worked out between social enterprises and the state.

In order to better view how the social contract is changed, I combine stakeholder theory (Freeman, 2010) and the postmodern lens of discursive order (Foucault, 2001; Versieren, 2016) in a combined analytical model. Social enterprises make changes to the social contract by the innovative ways they take and combine various stakeholder positions and the model allows me to track these changes. The analytical model was developed out of necessity. China has a unique, diverse, and rich culture that deserves to be approached with an open mind, yet many analyses of China are ideologically loaded or framed by orientalist historical perspectives. The emergence of social enterprises is recent and they are culturally ambiguous, both in China and the West. I needed an analytical model to compare social enterprises in different countries as well as to convey their precarious situation in China without any *a priori* normative stance blurring the view. The key issue in this book is not whether social enterprises contribute to a market or a socialist economy, to authoritarianism or democracy, but the myriad small ways in which they contribute to (re-)create Chinese society.

## The chronology

Chronologies are crucial to follow the political, and by implication economic, changes in China. It is common to use the name and years of office of the supreme rulers to distinguish between different eras and this is the principle used here. I will call them the Mao, the Deng, and the Xi era after the three rulers who each fronted a radical change in China's political economy (Fairbank & Goldman, 2006). The Mao era is named after Mao Zedong, the chairman of the CCP from 1949–1976. The Deng era is named after the paramount leader, Deng Xiaoping. It lasted from 1978 to 2013. That era includes the reign of Deng himself (1978–1989), and the time of the presidency of Jiang Zemin (1993–2003) and of Hu Jintao (2003–2013). The Xi era, after the current president, Xi Jinping, informally began in 2008 when he was designated as Hu Jintao's successor, but it is more common to refer to its beginning in 2013, when he was elected president.

The Mao era was a time of total social transformation. His political doctrine was rooted in anti-imperialism and Marxism-Leninism, to which was added political principles better suited to China's agrarian economy. His thoughts had wide global appeal, in particular in the Communist bloc (Cook, 2014). National policies were geared towards industrialisation and a socialist, planned economy as the means to realise a truly communist society. In this era, the civil wars that had devastated the country for a century came to an end with the proclamation of the People's Republic of China on October 1, 1949. China finally enjoyed full sovereignty; foreign powers no longer had any concessions. The industrialisation policies introduced in the Mao era aimed for swift transformation of the agrarian economy. To some extent, the policies succeeded, although the infamous Great Leap Forward Programmes for industrialisation in the 1950s led to a famine that killed millions of people (Dikötter, 2010, 2018). The surviving remnants of the form of civil society that had existed under the dynastic rule, the lineage-based villages, the landed gentry, and the business communities were dispossessed, sent to labour camps, or killed. New forms of reproductive and productive units were introduced in place of villages and urban communities. Civil society was subsumed under the state, and the state under the CCP. The Cultural Revolution of the 1960s and 1970s upended society even further, and the CCP barely managed to regain control (Koss, 2018). Along with the established social order, cultural and religious traditions, manifest in associations, customs or artefacts, were to a large extent destroyed. Much has survived in bits and pieces and is being put to good use in the present, but the fundamental reshaping of the political economy makes Chinese society before and after 1949 two very different social realities.

A different form of modernisation, colloquially known as the "Opening Up Reform" is the hallmark of the Deng era. Deng Xiaoping became the country's *de facto* leader in 1978. After taking over, Deng Xiaoping soon launched the "four Modernisations": Economy, agriculture, scientific and technological development, and national security. He redefined economic policy as a means to develop a socialist economy with Chinese characteristics. Part of the reform was the introduction of market economy mechanisms. One of the first attempts was the set-up of the now iconic Special Economic Zone, established in Shenzhen, Guangdong, in 1980. Today the area is known as the Silicon Valley of China. Other changes were restrictions that had kept "the bourgeoisie" from getting education, employment, or running for public office were rescinded. These reforms gradually re-established the division between state and civil society. The broadening of the possibilities for civil society and market participation steadily increased in the Deng era. During the presidency of Jiang Zemin, the private sector was gradually acknowledged and gained legal protection, and eventually, entrepreneurs and businesspeople could become CCP members. Under President Hu Jintao, new policies allowed non-governmental organisations to help the government deliver social services. Through these policy changes, local communities, grassroots players, and the business community have been formally recognised as parties to the social contract and may legitimately engage in Chinese statecraft. In the wake of these profound changes, social enterprise start-ups emerged in the early 2000s.

The current president, Xi Jinping, rapidly rose to become the country's supreme leader elected for life in 2018. His take on a socialist economy with Chinese characteristics is glossed in the expression of his "China dream," introduced in a speech in 2012. Contrasted with the "American dream," about individuals' rise from "rags to riches" through hard work, the "China dream" is said to reflect a yearning for prosperity and harmony more generally.[8] The Xi era is one of digitalisation and China has digitalised quicker and more broadly than anyone could have imagined, especially through the mobile (phone) economy (Ma & Lee, 2016). In the Xi era, the content of the social contract is changing again (Shambaugh, 2016). Digitalisation has profoundly affected social relations and opened for social enterprises in forms that were unknown in China until very recently, while more repressive policies silence civil society (Fu & Diestelhorst, 2020).

## The discursive topology

The topology, or discursively constituted social landscape, is not as easily discernible as the chronology. After all, this is an immensely complex social reality, as the young writer made so abundantly clear. In order to describe it with some form of clarity, I combine stakeholder theory, discourse theory, and the logic of the Chinese principle of *guanxi,* or connections. The original stakeholder theory appeared in the 1980s in the academic field of strategic management (Freeman, 2010). It was a period when private enterprises faced increasingly vocal opposition from sustainability-oriented community groups. Later, the stakeholder theory came to be widely used as a common framework in social science (Parmar et al., 2017). The key proposition in stakeholder theory was that groups other than shareholders have the right to influence corporate decisions in matters that directly influence them. Freeman identified the most common stakeholders and discussed how corporations could include them in deliberation over strategic decisions. Key stakeholder positions are illustrated in Figure 0.2.

As stakeholders have vested interest in a business, they also have knowledge and experiences that may help improve its performance, not only economically, but also in terms of environmental and social concerns. This theory redefines companies from purely economic to social units by showing the number of groups that have vested interests, or stakes, in their operations. The function of a company is the efficient management of resources, yes, but only through engagement with all stakeholders.

The stakeholder map of an organisation is composed of a limited number of corresponding social positions. Supplier corresponds with the customer, owner corresponds with the manager and so on. The positions gain cultural meaning from underlying ontological assumptions, which means they allot a discursive typology of roles and positions (Angenot, 2004), and through definitions, procedures and criteria for validation (Foucault, 2001). In every organisation, there is a range of such legally and culturally backed stakeholder positions that constitute social order.

The original stakeholder model only allows for subject positions. However, objects may very well be included. Like people, objects occupy cultural positions and from there mediate events, which means that they

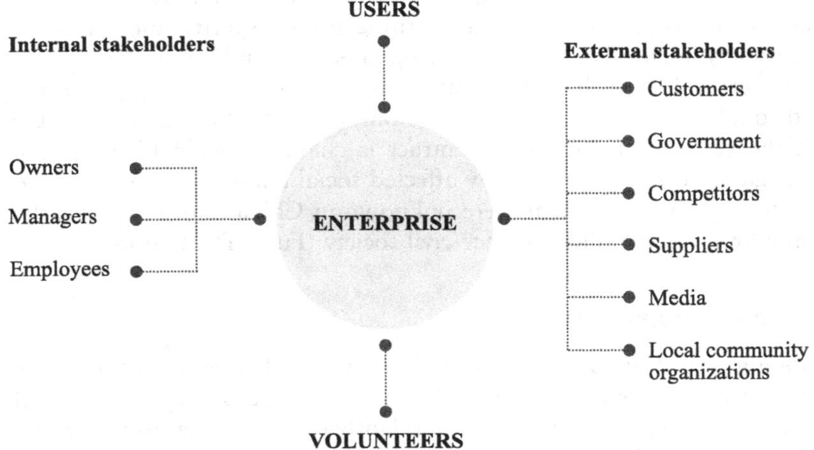


*Figure 0.2* Key stakeholders of an enterprise.

have agency. Not in the sense of conscious thought or free will but because they make a difference. Borrowing a term from actor–network theory, objects are "actants" (Callon, 1984). For example, a recurrent issue for the Swedish furniture chain IKEA's stores in China is that people spend hours of leisure time in the stores, lying on beds and dozing in chairs. IKEA has had a hard time figuring out how to respond. This is great for marketing purposes but the wear and tear on the goods is considerable.[9] This illustrates that understanding of the symbolic elements that place an object in the position of merchandise is not universally given but is culturally loaded. The Chinese are no strangers to shops, money, or merchandise. In this instance, IKEA's way of displaying the goods signalled free public space to the Chinese, like benches in a park, only much more comfortably indoors. Customers turned into consumers. At first, IKEA did not know how to respond to this literal interpretation of their display of goods until the company decided to see it as a marketing opportunity, which brought the whole matter safely into well-known market economy territory. No inherent quality in people or objects determines whether they become customers or commodities or what their price will be (Brøgger & Jevnaker, 2014).

Subject and object positions are not randomly related but gain specific meaning through their relations with what I call predicate positions. In a market transaction, price fills the predicate position. An object fills the position of merchandise and people the positions of suppliers and customers through the price mechanism. In voluntary associations, the social mission fills a predicate position. Usually composed only of a few words, it brings to life the desired outcome and gives meaning and order to the activities. Together, subject, object, and predicate positions make up a

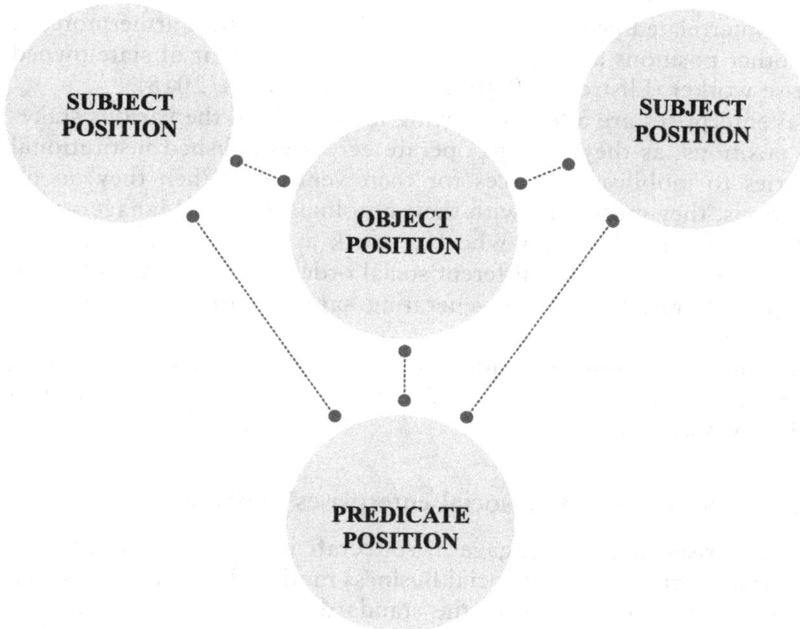


*Figure 0.3* Generic sociocultural configuration.

particular sociocultural configuration. Figure 0.3 illustrates the generic sociocultural configuration.

## *Guanxi* – a total social fact

China's political economy has been termed a "gift economy" because it is so dependent on *guanxi*; that is, transactions in reciprocal, informal social networks (Yan, 1996; Yan, 2002). The Chinese preoccupation with *guanxi* is well documented and attests to the function of socially mediated transactions that constitute Chinese society (Kipnis, 2012). Business connections are not constituted along functional lines as in Western enterprises but depend on *guanxi* (Tong, 2014). Birthplace, dialect, kin, party membership, alumni, and military service are often more relevant criteria for connecting with others for business purposes than functional, meritocratic criteria such as HR, finance, or marketing competence. Therefore, groups that would not have been included in the original stakeholder model need to be included in order to convey the social realities of social enterprises in China.

Studies of *guanxi* often concentrate mainly on the relations between people, but objects and predicates may very well be included. A review of the *guanxi* literature shows that it "can refer to the state of being related between two or more entities, be they animate or inanimate, concrete or abstract (e.g., between two concepts), and human or non-human, as networks of interrelated people" (Chen et al., 2004, p. 170). Furthermore, in China, other positions are more central; for example, that of state-owned enterprise worker (Elfstrom, 2020) or party cadre (Koss, 2018).

Social enterprises are adept at moving in and out of the various stakeholder positions, as they need to operate across established institutional boundaries to mobilise resources for their ventures. When they do fill the positions, they must cope with their ontological logic. Managers who insist that they are customers who buy work as a form of merchandise from suppliers create a very different social order than those who behave like employers responsible for generating safe conditions of work for the employees.

By moving in and out of positions or bringing a position into another configuration, social enterprises change the discursive topography in a myriad of ways.

## Special qualities of Chinese social enterprises' missions

Social enterprises in China engage in statecraft in different ways, which makes for a unique variety of social business models. Furthermore, social enterprises in China differ from the standard business school textbook models. They are as concerned with the conflict between profit and mission, and between doing good and doing well, as social enterprises in other countries. However, two aspects of their social mission set Chinese social enterprises apart. The first is that the conflict between being social and non-social is a more acute problem than the conflict between for-profit and social mission. The second is a foundational idea of cultivation: That economic development equals cultural development. Social enterprises in China place the quality of being at the heart of their endeavours in a unique manner.

### *Social inclusion*

The for-profit and social mission dilemmas that social enterprises in other countries struggle with are not as acute in China. Many micro-entrepreneurs who start schools or health services have no qualms about making money from them and would not call themselves social entrepreneurs. As long as they operate within the legal framework of their industry, making money from providing a social service is not seen as morally problematic. Rather the opposite. How can it be wrong to establish a viable business operation? This unproblematic blend of the social and commercial is a cultural distinction of social enterprises in China. As long as the enterprise can fund its operations solely from the surplus of commercial transactions, it may be a for-profit or a mission-oriented enterprise, or both, in whatever mix the owners and managers prefer. What would be next to impossible, though, is to establish an unsocial enterprise. That would be not only contrary to Party dictums, but to be withdrawn from *guanxi* relations.

The category of "unsocial" is mine, and I use it as a heuristic device to explain a particular condition in China, namely how people are defined by their social relations. In the West, the dominant idea is that people are individuals who do whatever they do out of rational, informed self-interest. Related to this axiom are ideas that self-interest is morally good and good for society somehow. Adam Smith is credited with the clearest expression of this idea but it has deeper roots (Strathern, 1992). According to this mindset, being individualistic or even egoistic should be the norm, especially in business. There is a limit to that of course. If too self-absorbed, a person could be diagnosed with a psychiatric condition, but in general, to be social is to be properly, recognisably self-interested. In this light, altruism becomes a problem, something out of the ordinary. Why would someone choose to put the interests of others above their own? Parents are expected to attend to their children's needs before their own, yes, but strangers? In China too, one would not be expected to do good to just any stranger. However, one is expected to place the interests of one's social relations, relatives, friends, and connections above one's own. This is why the avoidance of of being "unsocial" is so culturally important in China. To be regarded as unsocial is to disappear as a person or as an enterprise.

I emphasise the social not to imply that that people in China may not act egoistically or that people do not regard themselves as distinct beings, only that cultural norms about sociality are different from those in the West. This again influences what is culturally possible for social enterprises in China. Therefore, it becomes a problem for an enterprise to be defined as unsocial; that is, breaking the cultural rules of interaction. This is also why it is less problematic to make a profit. In China, there is little doubt about what it means to be unsocial but there are many ways to be social. The social, in this sense, necessarily must infuse every aspect of a social enterprise's operations.

### *Civilised society*

The second special quality of social enterprises in China is the care for the quality of being, for being civil. Social enterprises everywhere are started to meet social needs such as reducing poverty, school drop-out rates or discrimination, or improving health care services. There is an instrumental quality to the mission. What matters is what is done and its results: An improvement in the quality of human living conditions. At the same time, how the developmental process affects ways of being in the world is also important, so it is not this quality that is different. Social enterprises everywhere work to support the self-efficacy of their stakeholders or against discrimination of vulnerable groups. This is apparent from the recent emergence of global indicators to measure life quality, such as human dignity (the ability to lead a rewarding life) (Nussbaum, 2013), empowerment (Welzel, 2014), or happiness (Ura et al., 2012).

Social enterprises in China add similar but different existential-sentimental qualities to their social missions, best described as a particularly cultured version of being. Culture, in the broad sense of art, language, norms, civility, ethnicity, custom, and tradition, contributes to human cultivation in one form or other. Social enterprises in China aim to contribute to this broad cultural growth of people and society. One social entrepreneur said she started a social enterprise because her town was dying culturally. Although an outwardly prosperous town, its inhabitants did not have the knowledge and skills to participate in discussions about knowledge, language, philosophy, or ethics. There was education, but only to become a productive member of society, not to realise the full potential of being human.

This concern for the quality of being is remarkable for several reasons. First, it is a far cry from the productivist, social engineering perspectives that dominate the national social innovation policies (Mok et al., 2017). Second, care for the cultured version of the social is remarkable in the light of how far virtual sociality has come in China. China has the highest number of mobile Internet users in the world and e-commerce reaches the most remote corners of this vast country, while digital social control is the most severe. Still, even while living in the eye of the storm of intense digital sociality, at the same time, the Chinese have less control of their reputations they are ranked and classified by algorithms about which they have no knowledge (Ma & Lee, 2016). Third, it is remarkable in the light of how social "outliers" are viewed and treated. The poor, handicapped sick, minorities, and generally anyone who is challenged in any way, is kept out of sight or keeps out of sight, barely tolerated and seen as the problem of a family or group of peers (see, for example, Srinivas et al., 2020). As in other countries, the treatment of the marginalised is changing, not least through social innovation policy and social enterprises themselves but such efforts are still at the margins of mainstream society. Fourth, it is also remarkable in a country with a tradition for public humiliation as an acceptable punishment, in child rearing as well as in the treatment of criminals and political opponents (Chan et al., 2009; Zhang, 2014). Fifth, when social problems spring from central economic policy choices, some social enterprises, engage in what borders on political activism to improve the quality of life of those negatively effected. This is may lead to repercussions both for the enterprises and the beneficiaries.

## The following chapters

This book is divided into three parts and seven chapters.

Part 1, Overview, has two chapters on the global social enterprise movement as well as the emergence of social enterprises in China. Chapter 1 identifies three influential drivers of the global social enterprise movement and the ethos that infuse them: The counterculture movement, free marketeers, and the open-source community, all with strong roots in California and Silicon Valley. The main characteristics of the legal, financial, and institutional frameworks that are emerging around the world are also discussed in this chapter. The social enterprise movement in China is introduced in Chapter 2. Key drivers are China's social innovation and social policies. The emergent supportive infrastructure and forms of social enterprises are then discussed.

Part 2, Cases, consists of four empirical chapters. Chapters 3 to 5 present different types of social enterprises. The emphasis in each chapter is how the typical social enterprises mediates the particular sociocultural configurations dominant in its part of the political economy: the market economy, the modern economy, and the moral economy. Even in the current repressive climate, they manage to grow. In Chapter 6 these three types of enterprise are compared with three other types of organisations that are or were tasked with caring for people.

Chapter 3 tells the story of Disability Employment Works Ltd. (DEW), started in 2015. It operates in the international market sphere of China's political economy. DEW only employs people with disabilities. It is located in a special economic zone and is a sub-supplier to a number of foreign multinationals. It needs to collaborate with Chinese villagers in the form of the workers' families on the one hand and with the elite government-supported non-governmental organisations (GONGO) on the other, but otherwise has little to do with the government.

Chapter 4 is devoted to the Qushuo Academy, a private charitable enterprise started in 2012. It operates in the secular, modern society established in the Mao era. It aims to revitalise a small town and create a vibrant public sphere by providing teaching and meeting facilities. It has successfully mobilised parents and grandparents, public schools, party cadres, and foreign volunteers for its mission and is balancing precariously on the edge of the conflicting interests of the various stakeholders.

Chapter 5 tells the story of the Baisha Naxi Embroidery Institute, a commercial-cum-social venture started by a minority ethnic group in 2003. It operates in the remote west and the rapidly emerging tourist industry. It has restored an artisanal tradition of the Naxi ethnic group and its commercial wing is products for sale to tourists. Its social wing trains disabled youth from distant villages and helps them to set up training facilities at home. It collaborates closely with the government yet perpetuates its own distinct moral economy.

In Chapter 6, three typical social enterprises are compared with three other types of enterprises that take social responsibility: State-owned enterprises (SOE), rural economic cooperatives and faith-based organisations. While these are not defined as social enterprises proper, the comparison tests whether the pattern of stakeholder positions that the study of Chinese social enterprises uncovers is particular for the new type of social enterprises. If not, the model may be generalised to other areas of the political economy.

Part 3, Findings, consists of two concluding chapters. Chapter 7 discusses and sums up how the social enterprises alter the sociocultural configurations and thereby the content of the social contract. Five paradoxes and three lessons crucial when engaging in social entrepreneurship in China are discussed in Chapter 8.

## Notes

1 United Nation Development Programme. Human Development Reports. http://hdr.undp.org/en/content/latest-human-development-index-ranking.
2 British Council. The state of social enterprise in India. https://www.britishcouncil.org/sites/default/files/bc-report-ch4-india-digital_0.pdf, page 19.
3 British Council. The state of social enterprise in Kenya. https://www.britishcouncil.org/sites/default/files/state_of_social_enterprise_in_kenya_british_council_final.pdf, page 40.
4 Russia New Agency. July 26, 2020. Number of social enterprises amounts to around 50,000 in Russia in one year. https://tass.com/economy/1182483.
5 Letelier, L. February 2, 2021. Journey into Brazil's Social Sector (SSIR). https://ssir.org/articles/entry/journey_into_brazils_social_sector#
6 Kobro, L. (2019). Social enterprises and their ecosystems in Europe: Country fiche: Norway. In Publications Office of the European Union. http://op.europa.eu/en/publication-detail/-/publication/b93d3cf0–67cf-11e9-9f05-01aa75ed71a.
7 The battle against Salesforce is won, but what next for social enterprise? http://www.theguardian.com/social-enterprise-network/2012/sep/05/battle-salesforce-won-social-enterprise)
8 Chen, G. (2019). A Comparative Study on the Chinese Dream and the American Dream. 2nd International Seminar on Education Research and Social Science (ISERSS 2019), https://doi.org/10.2991/iserss-19.2019.146
9 Levin, Dan. August 26, 2016. Shh, it is naptime at IKEA in China. New York Times. https://www.nytimes.com/2016/08/27/world/what-in-the-world/shh-its-naptime-at-ikea-in-china.html. Assessed Dec. 23, 2020; Chen, Qin, August 2019. Chinese shoppers love napping at Ikea. Ikea says it is ok. https://www.inkstonenews.com/business/ikeas-china-head-says-you-can-nap-show-room/article/3024396. Accessed Dec. 23, 2020.

## References

Angenot, M. (2004). Social discourse analysis: Outlines of a research project. *The Yale Journal of Criticism*, *17*(2), 199–215. https://doi.org/10.1353/yale.2004.0008

Brøgger, B., & Jevnaker, B. H. (2014). The cultural production of commodities: Understanding the art and gaps of silent and seen design. *Society and Business Review*, *9*(2), 124–138. https://doi.org/10.1108/SBR-11-2013-0085

Bulpitt, J. (1986). The discipline of the new democracy: Mrs Thatcher's domestic statecraft. *Political Studies*, *34*(1), 19–39. https://doi.org/10.1111/j.1467-9248.1986.tb01870.x

Bøckmann, H. (2008). China today – and tomorrow? In M. Lie, R. Lund, G. H. Hansen, & H. Bøckman (Eds.), *Making it in China* (pp. 23-42). Høyskoleforlaget.

Callon, M. (1984). Some elements of a sociology of translation: Domestication of the scallops and the fishermen of St Brieuc Bay. *The Sociological Review*, *32*(S1), 196–233. https://doi.org/10.1111/j.1467-954X.1984.tb00113.x

Chan, S. M., Bowes, J., & Wyver, S. (2009). Chinese parenting in Hong Kong: Links among goals, beliefs and styles. *Early Child Development and Care*, *179*(7), 849–862. https://doi.org/10.1080/03004430701536525

Chen, C. C., Chen, Y.-R., & Xin, K. (2004). Guanxi practices and trust in management: A procedural justice perspective. *Organization Science*, *15*(2), 200–209. https://doi.org/10.1287/orsc.1030.0047

Cook, A. C. (Ed.). (2014). *Mao's Little red book: A global history*. Cambridge University Press.

Dikötter, F. (2010). *The tragedy of liberation: A history of the Chinese revolution, 1945–1957* (First U.S. Edition ed.). Bloomsbury Press.

Dikötter, F. (Ed.). (2018). *Mao's Great Famine – the History of China's most Devastating Catastrophe, 1958-1962*. Bloomsbury Press.

Durkheim, É. (2018). *Professional ethics and civic morals*. Routledge, Taylor & Francis Group.

Elfstrom, M. (2020). Holding the Government's Attention: State Sector Workers in China. In K. J. Koesel, V. J. Bunse, & J. C. Weiss (Eds.), *Citizens and the State in Authoritarian Regimes: Comparing China and Russia* (pp. 191–220). Oxford University Press.

Ellis, T. (2010). *The new pioneers: Sustainable business success through social innovation and social entrepreneurship*. Wiley.

Fairbank, J. K., & Goldman, M. (2006). *China: A new history* (2nd enl. ed.). Belknap Press of Harvard University Press.

Foucault, M. (2001). *The order of things: An archaeology of the human sciences* (Repr ed.). Routledge. (1966)

Freeman, R. E. (2010). *Strategic management: A stakeholder approach* (Reissue ed.). Cambridge University Press.

Fu, D., & Diestelhorst, G. (2020). Political opportunities for participation and China's leadership transition. In K. J. Koesel, V. Bunce, & J. C. Weiss (Eds.), *Citizens and the state in authoritarian regimes: Comparing China and Russia* (pp. 59–75). Oxford University Press.

Gåsemyr, H. J. (2017). Navigation, circumvention and brokerage: The tricks of the trade of developing NGOs in China. *The China Quarterly*, *229*, 86–106. https://doi.org/10.1017/S0305741016001557

Huybrechts, B., Defourny, J., Nyssens, M., Bauwens, T., Cuyper, P. D. E., Degavre, F., Hudon, M., Pongo, T., Rijpens, J., & Thys, S. (2016). Social Enterprise in Belgium: A diversity of Roots, Models and Fields (ICSEM Working Papers No. 27, Issue).

Kipnis, A. B. (Ed.). (2012). *Producing Guanxi: Sentiment, self, and subculture in a North China village*. Duke University Press.

Koss, D. (2018). *Where the party rules: The rank and file of China's communist state*. Cambridge University Press.

Kobro, L. (2019). Social enterprises and their ecosystems in Europe. Country Fiche Norway. Directorate General for Employment, Social Affairs and Inclusion. European Commission. https://op.europa.eu/en/publication-detail/-/publication/b93d3cf0-67cf-11e9-9f05-01aa75ed71a1.

Li, X., & Soobaroyen, T. (2021). Accounting, Ideological and Political Work and Chinese multinational operations: A neo-Gramscian perspective. *Critical Perspectives on Accounting*, *74*, 1–25. https://doi.org/10.1016/j.cpa.2020.102160

Letelier, L. (2012). Journey into Brazil's social sector. *Stanford Social Innovation Review*, 10, 1–5. https://ssir.org/articles/entry/journey_into_brazils_social_sector

Ma, W., & Lee, X. (2016). *China's mobile economy: Opportunities in the largest and fastest information consumption boom*. Wiley.

Minzner, C. (2019). *End of an era: How China's authoritarian revival is undermining its rise*. Oxford University Press.

Mok, K. H., Kühner, S., & Huang, G. (2017). The productivist construction of selective welfare pragmatism in China. *Social Policy & Administration*, *51*(6), 876–897. https://doi.org/10.1111/spol.12337

Nicholls, A. (2012). Postscript: The legitimacy of social entrepreneurship: Reflexive isomorphism in a pre-paradigmatic field. In B. Gidron & Y. Hasenfeld (Eds.), *Social Enterprises* (pp. 222–247). Palgrave Macmillan UK.

Nussbaum, M. C. (2013). *Creating capabilities: the human development approach* (First Harvard University Press paperback edition ed.). The Belknap Press of Harvard University Press.

O'Brien, K. J., & Li, L. (2006). *Rightful Resistance in Rural China*. Cambridge University Press. https://doi.org/10.1017/CBO9780511791086

Pan, Y. (2017). *Rural Welfare in China* (1st ed. 2017 ed.). Springer International Publishing: Imprint: Springer.

Parmar, B. L., Freeman, R. E., Harrison, J. S., Wicks, A. C., Purnell, L., & de Colle, S. (2017). Stakeholder theory: The state of the art. *Academy of Management Annals*, *4*(1), 403–445. https://doi.org/10.5465/19416520.2010.495581

Shambaugh, D. (2016). The illusion of Chinese power, in Shambaugh, D. (Ed.). *The China Reader*. Sixth edition (pp. 26-33). Oxford University Press.

Srinivas, M. L., Yang, E. L. J., Shrestha, P., Wu, D., Peeling, R. W., & Tucker, J. D. (2020). Social innovation in diagnostics: Three case studies. *Infectious Diseases of Poverty*, 9(1), Article 20. https://doi.org/10.1186/s40249-020-0633-6

Strathern, M. (1992). *After nature: English kinship in the late twentieth century*. Cambridge University Press.

Tong, C.-K. (Ed.). (2014). *Chinese business: Rethinking Guanxi and trust in Chinese business networks* (1st ed. 2014 ed.). Springer Singapore: Imprint: Springer.

Ura, K., Alkire, S., Zangmo, T., & Wangdi, K. (2012). *A Short Guide to Gross National Happiness Index*. The Centre for Bhutan Studies. https://opendocs.ids.ac.uk/opendocs/handle/20.500.12413/11807

Versieren, J. (2016). The moral foundations of Adam Smith's transitional society: Reappraising Foucault's representations of wealth and Marx's reconstruction of value theory. *Capital and Class*, *40*(3), 447–468. https://doi.org/10.1177/0309816816653893

Welzel, C. (2014). *Freedom rising: Human empowerment and the quest for emancipation*. Cambridge University Press.

Yan, Y. (1996). *The flow of gifts: Reciprocity and social networks in a Chinese village*. Stanford University Press.

Yan, Y. (2002). Unbalanced reciprocity: Asymmetrical gift giving and social hierarchy in rural China. In M. Osteen (Ed.), *The question of the gift: essays across disciplines* (pp. 67–84). Routledge.

Yu, L. (2020). The emergence of social entrepreneurs in China. *Journal of the International Council for Small Business*, *1*(1), 32–35. https://doi.org/10.1080/26437015.2020.1714359

Zhang, J. (2014). Understanding Chinese cultural child-rearing attitudes and practices. *NYS Child Welfare/Child Protective Services Training Institute*. https://digitalcommons.buffalostate.edu/cgi/viewcontent.cgi?article=1007&context=cwcpstriaininginstitute.

Zhang, W. (2017). The social enterprise movement. In Q. Jiang, L. Qian, & M. Ding (Eds.), *Fair Development in China* (pp. 135–166). Springer International Publishing.

Zhou, W., Zhu, X., Qiu, T., Yuan, R.,Chen, J., Chen, T. English language version edited by Evans, D.H. and translated by Ding, M. (2013). China Social Enterprise and Impact Investment Report. China Social Enterprise and Impact Investment Report. Shanghai University of Finance & Economics Social Enterprise Research Center, Peking University Center for Civil Society Studies, the 21st Century Social Innovation Research Center, and the University of Pennsylvania School of Social Policy & Practice. china-social-enterprise-and-investment-report-aug-2013-en.pdf.

# Part I

# Overview

# 1 The global social enterprise movement

The global social enterprise movement gained momentum in the early 2000s as social entrepreneurs, consultants and academics met at national and international workshops and conferences. What started as unconnected initiatives became a loosely connected mass of events and people, then a global movement. Many of the participants had been engaged in local voluntary work and social activism long before anyone had heard of a social enterprise. Three previous global movements, in particular, influenced the debates: Counterculture hippies, free marketeers, and the open-source community. People in the global social enterprise movement heartily disagreed among themselves about the right way to engage, while maintaining a sense of unity against those suspected of only being out to make a profit. However, the "do something good for you and society" ethos of earlier movements did not help resolve the problem of how to finance and run a viable business and what to do with the surplus. Thus, with the same zeal and energy that they debated the principles and started new ventures, people set out to establish an academic discipline and to develop new financial and regulatory infrastructures to support social entrepreneurs.

## Influential academics

Three influential academics published volumes and established institutions that spread the word about social entrepreneurship and gave it legitimacy. One pioneer was the late professor Gregory Dees, known as "the father of social entrepreneurship education." Professor Dees was central in establishing the Stanford Centre of Social Innovation, still one of the most respected knowledge hubs. He soon moved on to establish another influential knowledge hub, the Centre for Advancement of Social Entrepreneurship in the Fuqua School of Business at Duke University (Dees et al., 2002). Another pioneer was senior fellow Jed Emerson, "the father of impact investment." Jed Emerson coined the term "blended value," which made it possible to think about getting social and environmental, as well as financial returns, on investment. He was an innovator in the impact investment industry and connected with influential foundations and charities,

DOI: 10.4324/9780429282591-1

which have come to be increasingly important for the financing of social enterprises globally (Bugg-Levine & Emerson, 2011). A third firebrand and "the father of social entrepreneurship theory" was university lecturer Alex Nicholls. With support from the Palo Alto-based world-leading social enterprise Skoll Foundation he was central in establishing the Skoll Centre for Social Entrepreneurship at the Said Business School, Oxford University. He was also editor of an influential book that brought together other leading scholars and activists (Nicholls, 2008). The same year as Nicholl's edited volume, a summary of research findings and validation of key was published (Light, 2008). It was a first, in what has become a vast body of literature (Hota et al., 2020). In the next decade, social entrepreneurship and innovation centres were established at universities and colleges all over the world and research soared.

## Pioneer social entrepreneurs

Even though the global social enterprise movement took shape in the early 2000s, there were similar experiments much earlier. These were unique and singular efforts by devoted individuals. Bill Drayton was the first to use the term social entrepreneur. As early as 1981, he got leave from McKinsey to start Ashoka, a global network in support of individual social entrepreneurs (Bornstein, 2006). According to Bornstein, Ashoka started because Bill Drayton wanted to support three social entrepreneurs he had met as part of his consultancy work. One was a primary school teacher in India with a new pedagogy for teaching poor children how to protect the environment. The second was an engineer in Brazil who had developed a sun-fueled electric pump. It provided poor farmers who could not afford to hook up to the public grids with water to irrigate their fields. The third was a nurse in South Africa who developed a training program for nursing hidden-away AIDS patients in their homes. All three had found a solution to a social problem, but none had the financial means or network to reach out beyond the local level. The social mission of Ashoka was to provide individual social entrepreneurs with the means to scale up their enterprises. Today it operates in over 90 countries (www.ashoka.org).

Another iconic figure is Muhammad Yunus, who scaled up microfinance and made it acceptable in the mainstream finance industry (www.muhammadyunus.org/). A social entrepreneur himself, Yunus was awarded the Nobel Peace prize in 2006 for his efforts in this area. Starting in the 1970s, he made use of age-old insurance or credit schemes (tontine arrangements) that enabled people to pool their resources and share risk. Yunus's Grameen Bank provided women too poor to qualify for bank loans with enough credit to buy equipment to set up their own businesses. Yunus's microfinance scheme has since financed numerous other social enterprises and today microfinance is a product offered by many commercial banks.

Things were happening in other areas as well. Coined in 1987, the term "sustainable development" was made famous by the then Norwegian prime minister Gro Harlem Brundtland. Its inclusion of future generations in calculations about development gains altered the way of thinking about development (Brundtland, 1990). The idea of corporate social responsibility (CSR) pressured large corporations to consider their responsibility to wider society (Midttun, 2013). The concept of stakeholders, discussed in the Introduction, showed corporations how they could go about changing their practices, as did advocates of the *triple bottom line* (Elkington, 1999).

## The ethos

The combination of support for democracy, human rights and market ethos in the global movement is a legacy of earlier attempts at changing society. These influences overlapped, to some extent, and were definitely contradictory. While there were many, below is an overview according to three main types: The counterculture movement, free marketeers, and the open-source community. These did not appear simultaneously but in sequence. One shaped the other, to some extent, but each constituted a social force of its own. A brief sketch of the particularities of the cultural heritage of the global movement will bring out its key differences from the Marxist-Leninist-Maoist ideology it met when it reached China.

### *The anti-authoritarian counterculture movement*

Social entrepreneurship was a late bloomer in the global hub of entrepreneurship and innovation culture that emerged in Silicon Valley, the southern part of the area surrounding San Francisco in California. Its key advantage was a decentralised, collaborative institutional pattern (Saxenian, 2007), which it had inherited from the counterculture movement of the 1960s and 1970s. As early as the 1950s, and when the USA took over from Europe as the global economic superpower, large amounts of public funds poured into the area. The result was world-leading technological innovations in electronics and telecommunication. A steady stream of private investors looking for promising start-ups commercialised the new technologies. Foreign entrepreneurs gathered to learn and to launch their own ventures, bringing new ideas back home. New ways of supporting economic development were tried out in this intensely experimental climate.

At the time, political changes were also reshaping the geopolitical order. China was in the grip of the Cultural Revolution and Africa saw the end of colonisation. In South America Marxist-Leninist guerrillas emerged and tensions were growing within the Eastern Bloc. The icy atmosphere of the cold war had thawed slightly, and the popular fear of atomic war and environmental degradation was increasing. Why do I give priority to a cultural phenomenon like the counterculture when new technologies and political orders were in the making? Because it brought forth a new mindset. According to one of the few thorough insider analyses, it was cultural change in action (Anders, 1990). The movement happened through new forms of artistic expression, new blends of religious and philosophical belief systems, and experiments with alternative social and economic life arrangements. Civil rights marches, "sod brotherhoods" to nurture the environment, women's rights, world peace, all surfaced as social missions among the various groups and communities that constituted the movement. The counterculture opened up for alternative thinking and living. In its heyday in the 1960s and 1970s, the counterculture was either seen as a community of self-indulgent, irresponsible individuals or innovative freedom-seekers. Whatever the judgment, its impact on a whole generation is undisputed and marks a watershed between the post-war generation and the freewheeling hippies (Anderson, 1995). The Californian counterculture was a leading force for intellectual innovation and placing liberation and empowerment on the global agenda. Furthermore, the counterculture movement has left an anti-authoritarian legacy that is also still apparent in the social entrepreneurship movement.

### *Free marketeers*

Free market, libertarian ideas appeared alongside new technological breakthroughs in the 1980s, again with the epicentre in Silicon Valley. Free marketeers were ideologically preoccupied with the market as a better mechanism to ensure human development and freedom than states. This resonated well with the push for technological innovation already dominant in Silicon Valley. In a way, free marketeers secularised a utilitarian ethos, the Protestant ethic that Weber found so crucial for the emergence of capitalism, the "from rags to riches through hard work" dream of the early settlers to America (Nackenoff, 1994). One ideological compass was provided by the Austrian school of economics, promoting "creative destruction" as the vehicle for economic growth (Schumpeter & Stiglitz, 2010). The main idea is that incumbent firms do not generate economic change. They maintain the status quo. However, the incumbent's market position is destroyed by cheaper or better products and services brought to the market by the creative entrepreneurship and innovation of start-ups. The role of governments is to deregulate the economy and let go of central planning, while markets will regulate themselves. Even better, markets are in the hands of economists and business people who know how to maximise profit and generate the largest possible good for the largest number of people. Against this background, free marketeers set out to start businesses.

Governments at the time were affected by the same kinds of aspirations and were busy laying the groundwork for economic globalisation and market liberalisation. The European Union is a good example, with its call for the four freedoms: "the free flows of goods, capital, services and people," and the need to adjust national legislation accordingly. Other supranational bodies were established or gained strength and The World Trade Organisation (WTO) made headway. A number of pan-state development banks required market liberalisation to provide credit, and free trade agreements were established between countries, facilitating a rapidly increasing flow of economic transactions. Multinational corporations boosted economic growth and contributed to the emergence of global supply chains, economic behemoths that controlled the flow of goods and services from production to customer, regardless of the country of operation.

In the intense redesign of the global economic order, free marketeers were local firebrands, anarchists, and libertarians, exploring the possibility of economic democracy through start-ups. They were as opposed to the establishment as the counterculture activists two decades earlier but less sceptical about both capitalism and communism (Chartier & Johnson, 2011).

### *The open-source community*

The third main influence to be mentioned here is the entrepreneurial culture of the information technology industry in Silicon Valley. This area was a technological innovation hub long before the time of personal computers. Actually, the vision of personal computing was a child of the counterculture movement: "It is within this same population of rebels and drop-outs that we can find the inventors and entrepreneurs who helped lay the foundations of the California computer industry" (Roszak, 1986, p. 5). Personal computing was a way to democratise information technology, make it available to everyone. The rapid development of new technology not only brought forth personal computing, but the connectivity of the hardware and software that has made possible the digitalisation of the economy. In line with the counterculture ethos of liberation and empowerment, technology was not seen as a merely neutral instrument but as a way of living that should be available to all.

Investments from governments and large corporations were also crucial for the innovation drive of information technology. Silicon Valley, however, has become known for supporting "garage entrepreneurs," whose start-ups have become large corporations: Apple, Facebook, Spotify, Airbnb, Twitter. Openness and access for all is still a unique aspiration in the digital economy and was the thinking behind the world wide web (www). This was to be a virtual space where information can be shared has protocols, addresses and other mechanisms for connecting various data sources and making them generally accessible. In the words of the "inventor" of the www, "I told people that the web was like a market economy ...What they do need ... are a few practices everyone has to agree to, such as the currency used for trade, and the rules of fair trading" (Berners-Lee & Fischetti, 1999, p. 36). Many attempts to monopolise the web, for profit or political reasons, have been resisted. A consortium of paying members, governments, research institutions, corporations and organisations collaborate to keep the new communication infrastructures open and available. This is a club-like structure. Members pay a considerable fee to join, but the institution is governed through a variety of participatory and consultative mechanisms. This organisational innovation is a blend of counter culture, market, and open-source mechanisms. Social enterprises were quick to make use of the new technologies. Some social entrepreneurs used open-source platforms to explore new markets, others to establish their businesses, support networks, and find partners. Slowly, many diverse initiatives were consolidated and the social enterprise movements globalised.

## New supporting infrastructures

Supporting infrastructures are still in the making, diverse and disconnected, but much has been achieved nevertheless. After the first years of heady experimentation, social entrepreneurs began to look for more permanent management solutions. The idea of social enterprises as a distinct kind of company took hold. The idea was not the brainchild of one inventor in particular, but the outcome of many efforts to find practical solutions in the midst of idealistic fervour.

Two infrastructures in support of social enterprises are emerging at present, one regulatory and one financial. They vary between countries and regions depending on the structure of the political economy and welfare system but they are transnational and interconnect in various ways. Some have emerged to counter the dark side of social entrepreneurship but, mostly, they are based on investors' and grant givers' needs for information and control. Since they play a significant role in freeing up capital for social enterprises and increasing their legitimacy, the story of the global movement is incomplete without them.

### *Forms of social enterprise*

In the early days, no country had separate legislation for social enterprises. Some had a distinct legal company form that came close, such as a cooperative, ideal limited company or social benefit corporation. The problem was that none of them quite fit with the purpose and mission of many social entrepreneurs. Not worrying too much about legal fine print, social entrepreneurs mixed and blended the different organisational forms available in their countries. All states require commercial ventures to register or be certified by a public authority in one way or the other. Some entrepreneurs simply registered a commercial venture. Other social entrepreneurs with experiences as volunteers or aid workers, mobilised participants to form a voluntary association or a network. In some countries, voluntary associations are required to register, while in others they are not. Social entrepreneurs soon found that their choice of organisational form mattered for what they could actually do; at least if they wanted to continue their venture legally. There were taxes and VAT to consider, labour laws, and health and safety requirements. Having a social mission, doing good, was not enough. One had to prove it by operating the enterprise responsibly as well. The initial drive to start social enterprises was very much a bottom-up process and social entrepreneurs learned from each other in increasingly global networks, supported by research findings and consultants specialising in social enterprise management. It was a vast disorganised laboratory. It also had a dark side, as the following example shows.

An early social network in many countries was organised as a local trade exchange system. Known as LETS, it was a well-organised system of local micro-markets organised by the network. Participants could sell their second-hand items at regular intervals and some sold organic food directly to consumers. There were a number of LETS platforms available at the time. Some, like the Norwegian one I belonged to in the 1990s, used money, while others used currency such as labour or grain. Deals were done beforehand, through an early digital messaging system. First, the seller described the item and asked for a price. Then the buyer paid through a LETS account and collected the items at the market. It was also possible to do the actual exchange at the market. Either way, the LETS kept the ledgers, organised the markets and deducted a small fee for the service. At first, the ledgers were handwritten and, apart from the digital bulletin boards, people interacted mainly face to face or on the phone. After having lived abroad for some time, when I returned to the LETS site there was only a remnant of the earlier vigorous community left. I never found out what had happened, but pieced together enough information to guess. With the new open-source software, the ledgers had been digitised. As the system was a kind of clearing house for financial flows in all the local markets, digitalisation meant centralisation of large sums of money. The founder of that particular LETS had become immensely rich and left the system. Besides a few advertisements from die-hard participants still using the exchange system, the group webpage was flooded with advertisements for digital gambling outlets. The social platform had been hijacked and there were no regulatory mechanisms except social control, which apparently had not worked.

As stories about how individuals used the social enterprise format to enrich themselves circulated in the social entrepreneurship community, the lack of legal protection became clear. In line with the dominant anti-authoritarian ethos and the quest for economic democracy, idealists promptly set out to devise infrastructure solutions. The most radical solutions aimed to overthrow existing political economies. Others chose instead to hitch on to mechanisms already in place to regulate business. Among them was the B Corporation (B Corp) institution established in 2006 in the USA. It has since spread globally and made an impact on national legal frameworks regulating social enterprises. As such, it is a good illustration of how parts of the social enterprise movement are maturing into a social industry.

The B Corporation, a classification society, was established by three social entrepreneurs. The first 82 companies were certified as B Corps in 2007. In 2021, there were nearly 4,000 in 71 countries (bcorporation.net). To be certified, a company must supply its charter and business idea for assessment by B Lab, another company in the group. The enterprise must also document that it has incorporated the interests of all stakeholders and the environment into its constitution and management system. The company has to be registered as a legitimate business in its country of registration and the specific legal requirements depend on the regulatory framework in the country of registration. The B Corp may also assist with business modelling, management philosophy, and impact assessment tools and analytics, for which there are separate fees. The B Corp itself is not at all government based but depends on market finance and governance. Certified companies can display the B Corp logo on their sites and marketing material.

In some countries that have adopted the B Corp standard, companies applying for B Corp certification are legally required to change their constitution. In others, there is a publicly recognised B Corp Agreement they can apply for but no national legislative requirements. A few countries require B Corps to include triple bottom line reporting in their charters. As the B Corp example shows, regulatory infrastructure is in the making. At present, only Belgium, Colombia, Italy, the Netherlands, the United Kingdom, and a number of states in the USA acknowledge social enterprises as a distinct legal company form.

### *Rating and analytics*

Another mechanism for regulating social enterprises is to measure and share information about their social impact. Documenting the effects of their initiatives soon became a key challenge for social enterprises. While the tools to measure economic results were well developed, similar tools to assess social impact were not readily available. Some help came from evaluation methods already used by grant-giving charities and the foreign aid industry. The problem of how to assess the results of a single social enterprise remained. Social problems have many causes and exactly what solved a problem is hard to pin down. Hence, if there was an increase in literacy levels in a group or a reduction in the number of high school dropouts, it was hard for a social enterprise to claim responsibility for the good outcome. It may have contributed, but how and by how much was hard to assess.

Adding to the difficulty of precisely assessing impact is the fact that social change takes time, is incremental, and depends on the voluntary participation of beneficiaries. Social enterprises have many different stakeholders and finding a set of indicators relevant for all is a challenge. Beneficiaries need to know what is in it for them to engage with a social enterprise. Charities and governments want to know their funds reach their targets. Managers and investors in particular need input to make decisions that make the most of available resources. The need for indicators and ways to account for resources used and their outcomes was urgent. The solution was to latch on to new standards, rating agencies and certification bodies that emerged to measure the sustainability of investment vehicles.

One response to the need for standards was the Global Reporting Initiative (GRI) Inc. established in 1997 after calls for more corporate transparency following the Exxon Valdez oil spill in Alaska (www.globalreporting.org). The first version of its guidelines was launched in 2000. In 2006, a group of social entrepreneurs and socially concerned investors met to work out more specific social impact measurements. According to B Analytics, a company in the B Corp ecosystem, the participants based their work on three key sources.[1] There were the GRI guidelines, a how-to manual by two social entrepreneurs (Cohen & Warwick, 2006) and the Stanford National Capital Project on responsible investment.[2] The same year, a number of activist investors contesting the shareholder primacy theory, started another B Corp entity, B Lab, a rating agency that would certify B Corps, according to the newly developed Global Impact Investment Rating Standard (GIIRS).

Over the years, a number of other rating agencies have appeared. Sustainalytics, a conglomerate of investors and rating agencies (https://www.sustainalytics.com/about-us/#History) and the Sustainability Accounting Standards Board (https://www.sasb.org/about/) were other early adopters in 2009 and 2011 respectively. The standards and rating agencies make up a voluntary regulatory regime. Rating agencies and sustainability consultancies have since blossomed, yet without anything like the www clarity on regulatory mechanisms. There is fierce competition between various contenders for the best, global standard. If less coherent than the digital technology industry, they have certainly managed to change the mindset of international business, paving the way for broader and more inclusive strategies and making it easier for social enterprises to document their results.

### *The term Impact investment*

In 2007, the Rockefeller Foundation invited a number of associates to a first gathering and launched the term "impact investment" (Bugg-Levine & Emerson, 2011). It was one of the most influential accounts of the emergence of impact investment. In 2009, the Global Impact Investment Network was launched (thegiin.org). Its Annual Impact Investor Survey provides the most up-to-date knowledge on impact investment around the globe. They combined the earlier standards to create a coherent Impact

Reporting & Investment Standard (IRIS) used for the Annual Impact Investors report. In 2011, nine impact investment funds passed the GIIRS test and were rated for the first time.

### *Incubators and social venture capital*

In tandem with drives to establish rating and investment vehicles, new institutions for connecting investors and social entrepreneurs emerged all over the world. They came in a variety of shapes and provided different services for social entrepreneurs. Villgro was established in 2001 in India. Its programmes include support for green agriculture, family planning, health, biotech, and water management. It collaborates with national NGOs, public bodies and research institutions. The major part of its operations are in India but it also supports social entrepreneurs in Kenya, the Philippines and the USA (villgro.org).

SoCapGlobal, a US-based company, arranged its first physical event in 2008. It has since continued as a mediating digital platform (socapglobal.com). It provides scholarships for social entrepreneurs, social media outlets and volunteering opportunities. The Impact Investment Exchange (IIX) was established in Singapore in 2011 (iixglobal.com/). It supports female micro-entrepreneurs, especially in the Pacific and Asia and founder Professor Dureen Shahnaz was awarded the Oslo Business for Peace award in 2017.[3] Spring Impact, a UK-based company with operations across the globe has an Ashoka-like business idea, but instead of supporting individuals, it helps social enterprises scale up their business (springimpact.org). The SoCentral opened in Norway in 2016. Housed in the old headquarters of a commercial bank, it serves as a multipurpose venue for social and cultural entrepreneurs in Norway and operates a digital platform for Nordic social entrepreneurship (socentral.no/English). In Nigeria, Babban Gona was established in 2012 to attract youth to farming rather than warfare (https://babbangona.com). It is a for-profit company but, due to its mission and social impact, received the prestigious Skoll award for social entrepreneurship in 2017 (skoll.org/organisation/babban-gona).

Numerous well established foundations and public institutions also support social entrepreneurship. As these have less decentralised and collaborative governance structures, they are more suspected of serving their own interests. However, there can be no doubt as to the role they play among social entrepreneurs that qualify for their assistance. The USA-based Bill and Melinda Gates Foundation provides direct support to social entrepreneurs and indirect support through social entrepreneurship programmes, together with other charitable organisations (gatesfoundation.org). The UK-government institution, the British Council, provides social entrepreneurs with training and networks and the establishment with research and analyses (britishcouncil.org/society/social-enterprise). The German Bertelsmann Stiftung supports social entrepreneurs in its home country, as well as in India and China (bertelsmann-stiftung.de).

Although poorly connected and occasionally competing, these institutions all provide an invaluable framework for social entrepreneurs. Strategic manoeuvring for access to resources is necessary for any social entrepreneur but, as a better-developed set of institutions become established, they do not to spend resources on establishing supportive infrastructures, as the first generation of social enterprises had to do.

### *From micro-finance to big capital*

Muhammad Yunus's microfinance business model emerged in the 1980s. Decades later, big finance entered the scene together with government and international development institutions. In 2009, the United Nations (UN) launched a platform where stakeholders could explore what a social stock exchange would require to work. Today its initiatives are linked to the 17 UN sustainability development goals (SDF) and the Environment, Social and Governance (ESG)-criteria (sseinitiative.org) that measure the sustainability of companies' operations (Chhichhia, 2015). In 2013, the then prime minister of the UK announced the establishment of the G8 social investment task force, setting up national advisory boards in the eight participating nations.[4] In 2015, the Organisation for Economic Co-Operation and Development (OECD), with its 37 member countries and projects in more than 100 countries, launched its report on social investment.[5] The International Capital Market Association (ICMA) agreed on a set of Green Bond Principles (GBP) in 2014 and Social Bond Principles (SBP) in 2016 (icma.org). This enabled stock exchanges to have separate lists for green and social investment vehicles. A new financial instrument followed: The sustainability bond. They finance projects that aim to solve environmental problems such as global warming (green bonds) or welfare problems (social bonds). In April 2020, at a much-publicised launch, the first social bond of the African Development Bank, "Fight Covid-19," was listed on the London Stock Exchange's sustainable bond market. It was the largest social bond ever to be issued in the capital markets.[6]

Social stock exchanges (SSE), on the other hand, are not well developed. An early version was tried out in Brazil in 2003. A few years later, Kenya was reported to be the first country to open a social stock exchange, small and private, but still a platform specifically for social enterprises to access capital. South Africa and Brazil also have social exchange trading platforms. Larger social exchanges, of sorts, are available in Canada, the UK, the USA and Singapore (Chhichhiai, 2015; Wendt, 2017). After assessing the status, one study concludes that impact investment is maturing, but that "well-developed regulation and rules of governance are thus essential for ensuring the integrity of SSEs, and by extension, the impact economy as a whole" (Wendt, 2017, p. 40). In the last few years, a number of crowdfunding platforms have also become available for non-professional social investors.

### *Crowdfunding*

Crowdfunding is when many small-scale investors pool their resources. Microfinance is a kind of crowdfunding, only it is based on groups of people who meet regularly. The crowd is anonymous. Crowdfunding platforms emerged along with the digitalisation of the economy and especially the mobile economy that gave users easy access to digital platforms. These platforms made it possible for social entrepreneurs to reach out to a wider audience with their projects and offered a new way for socially minded people to contribute. Instead of channelling funds via voluntary associations, they would go directly to the social entrepreneur, with a small fee deducted by the platform owner. The platform owner provides the infrastructure for the sharing of information and secure transfer of funds. Crowdfunding platforms differ. Some are open for social as well as commercial projects (kickstarter.com), while others are limited to social projects (bolsasocial.com). Some let contributors pay a small sum each month (teaming.net) but it is more common to define the sum needed to start the venture and limit the call period. Some target companies (globalgiving.org), but it is more common to target private individuals. Social entrepreneurs may provide a "dividend" in the form of a product, an event or other forms of non-financial paybacks – if the venture succeeds.

### *Volunteers*

Traditionally, many NGOs depended on volunteers to provide services. This was a big saving on labour costs. Volunteers were not paid or only had their costs covered but then the NGO did not demand payment for its services either. Unlike employees, volunteers were free to come and go. How to best deal with volunteers became a special management skill and the more professional the NGOs became, the more professional their treatment of volunteers. When social entrepreneurs entered the scene, in many instances they were treated as volunteers, much to their dismay. Public agencies in particular, but also some companies, continued to treat social entrepreneurs as free labour, a saving on resources that could be used for other purposes. In the beginning, when the social enterprise was not a legitimate organisation form or known at all, these organisations had difficulty convincing their customers that they were not volunteers in the traditional sense but intended to provide services for a fee.

## From movement to industry

From the early beginnings of the 2000s until today, the movement has gradually developed more into a social industry with specific standards, financial instruments and representative bodies, of sorts. Social entrepreneurs and their supportive infrastructure operate as a decentralised, collaborative ecosystem, which has not been co-opted by any state, public body or corporation. Its ethos is still anti-authoritarian, advocating economic democracy, liberation, and empowerment. This diverse movement brought its transformative power to China, providing its particular pushes and pulls on social entrepreneurs who had to balance them with quite different domestic pushes and pulls.

## Notes

1 https://b-analytics.net/content/our-history.
2 https://naturalcapitalproject.stanford.edu/
3 https://businessforpeace.no/oslo-business-for-peace-honourees-2017-announced/
4 https://www.gov.uk/government/groups/social-impact-investment-taskforce
5 https://www.oecd.org/social/social-impact-investment.htm.
6 https://www.londonstockexchange.com/discover/news-and-insights/fixed-income-pulse-african-development-bank-group-3-billion-fight-covid-19-social-bond?lang=en

## References


Anders, J. (1990). *Beyond counterculture: The community of Mateel.* Washington State University Press.

Anderson, T. H. (Ed.). (1995). *The movement and the sixties: Protest in America from Greensboro to Wounded Knee* (5th ed.). Oxford University Press.

Berners-Lee, T., & Fischetti, M. (1999). *Weaving the Web: The original design and ultimate destiny of the World Wide Web by its inventor* (1st ed.). HarperSanFrancisco.

Bornstein, D. (2006). *How to Change the World: Social Entrepreneurs and the Power of New Ideas.* Oxford University Press.

Brundtland, G. H. (1990). *Our common future. World Commission of Environment and Development.* Oxford University Press.

Bugg-Levine, A., & Emerson, J. (2011). *Impact investing: Transforming How We Make Money While Making a Difference.* Jossey-Bass.

Chartier, G., & Johnson, C. W. (Eds.). (2011). *Markets not capitalism: Individualist anarchism against bosses, inequality, corporate power, and structural poverty.* Minor Compositions.

Chhichhia, B. (Jan. 8, 2015). The Rise of Social Stock Exchanges (SSIR). Standford Social Innovation Reviewhttps://ssir.org/articles/entry/the_rise_of_social_stock_exchanges

Cohen, B., & Warwick, M. (2006). *Values-driven business: How to change the world, make money, and have fun* (1st ed.). Berrett-Koehler Publishers; Publishers Group West [distributor].

Dees, J. G., Emerson, J., & Economy, P. (2002). *Strategic tools for social entrepreneurs: Enhancing the performance of your enterprising nonprofit.* Wiley.

Elkington, J. (1999). *Cannibals with forks: the triple bottom line of 21st century business* (Reprint ed.). John Wiley & Son Ltd.

Hota, P. K., Subramanian, B., & Narayanamurthy, G. (2020). Mapping the Intellectual Structure of Social Entrepreneurship Research: A Citation/Co-citation

Analysis. *Journal of business ethics, 166*(1), 89–114. 10.1007/s10551-019-04129-4

Light, P. C. (2008). *The search for social entrepreneurship*. Brookings Institution Press.

Midttun, A. (Ed.). (2013). *CSR and beyond: A Nordic perspective*. Cappelen Damm Akademisk.

Nackenoff, C. (1994). *The Fictional Republic: Horatio Alger and American Political Discourse*. Oxford University Press.

Nicholls, A. (2008). *Social Entrepreneurship: New Models of Sustainable Social Change* (A. Nicholls, Ed.). Oxford University Press.

Roszak, T. (1986). *From Satori to Silicon Valley. San Francisco and the American Counterculture*. Don't Call it Frisco Press.

Saxenian, A. (2007). *The new argonauts: Regional advantage in a global economy* (First Harvard University Press paperback edition). Harvard University Press.

Schumpeter, J. A., & Stiglitz, J. E. (2010). *Capitalism, socialism and democracy: With a new introduction by Joseph E. Stiglitz*. Routledge.

Wendt, K. (2017). Social Stock Exchanges – Democratization of Capital Investing for Impact [SSRN Scholarly Paper](ID 3021739). https://papers.ssrn.com/abstract=3021739https://papers.ssrn.com/sol3/papers.cfm?abstract_id=3021739

# 2 The social enterprise movement in China

It is an open question whether the social enterprise movement in China will continue to be a vibrant movement or is withering in the current more repressive climate. The Chinese movement is as multifaceted and unruly as the global one but its diversity springs from different sources. One is the fact that social innovation is a tool in the government's policies for economic development rather than an end in itself. Another is how social policy reforms opened opportunities for the grassroots to assist the government in providing social and community services. With the Deng era reforms, the legalised private sector generated new business models and a supportive infrastructure for many social enterprises. The hegemonic CCP is everywhere but this does not mean that there is no space for collaboration or even resistance, rather the polity provides a configuration of relations that social entrepreneurs must carefully manage. Recent policy changes are, in some respects, more repressive towards social enterprises and in others more inclusive.

## The number and types of social enterprises in China

The concept of social entrepreneurship was first publicly used in China in 2004 at several international conferences supported by international institutions (Yu, 2020; Yu, 2011; Zhou et al., 2013) and volumes that helped shape the global movement were translated into Chinese the following years (Zhang, 2017). These new tools and possibilities for economic development meant it did not take long for the Chinese to become eager social entrepreneurs.

The actual number of social enterprises in China is uncertain for the same reasons that the global number is uncertain. Many social enterprises do not survive their first year of operation, many are not registered and those that do register turn up in various company guises. In China, social enterprises may register either as commercial enterprises or as social organisations. Some even register as both (Jia & Desa, 2020; Yu, 2016). Even if uncertain, it is still useful to examine the most recent figures in the national statistics to

DOI: 10.4324/9780429282591-2

get an idea of their number. They come in two main forms: Social organisations and private businesses.

In 2018, the number of registered social organisations was about 800,000, or 4% of the total number of legal enterprises. Social organisation is a loose term for all kinds of non-governmental organisations with a social mission, such as mutual help groups, trade associations, private schools, religious associations, foreign NGOs, social enterprises, para-governmental, and private-public partnerships.

In the same period, the number of business enterprises was about 17.7 million units (minus state-owned enterprises). As there is little reluctance to combine for-profit and social mission, and because of special types of township and village enterprises and e-commerce-based businesses, the number of units that operate as social enterprises probably makes up a significant number of the registered private enterprises, even if their percentage of the private businesses total is negligible. Commercial interests dominate private business in China, as in the rest of the world. What sets China apart is the overwhelming dominance of government and collectively owned units. Also, many government bodies, especially at the village level, fulfil functions that are covered by non-profit private enterprises or non-governmental organisations in other countries. With these caveats in mind, it is still worthwhile to look at the national statistics (See Table 2.1).

In the national statistics, social organisations are further subdivided into three different types: Foundations, non-enterprise units run by NGOs, and social organisations (see Table 2.2). The foundations play an important role as an infrastructure for the social enterprise movement but are not themselves social enterprises. They make up just above 7,000 units. The non-enterprise units are where most social enterprises are likely to be found. Such units are engaged in many social services, such as first aid, education, health and social services, sports, culture, and food initiatives. They make up about 450,000 units, while the remaining number of social organisations is about 366,000.

Numbers from a study of NGOs in Beijing, Shanghai, and Sichuan indicate that about 10% of non-enterprise units operate in only three

*Table 2.1* Number of legal enterprises in China

| | *Legal enterprises* * | *Domestic funded enterprises* ** | *Social organizations* *** |
|---|---|---|---|
| Total number | 22 09 092 | 17 698 248 | 817 360 |

* 2017. Table 1.5. Number of legal entities by sector. China Statistical Yearbook 2019.

** 2017. Table 1.8. Number of business entities by region and status of registration, 17 830 471 with state-owned enterprises (133 233). China Statistical Yearbook 2019.

*** 2018. Table 22:24. Statistics on social organizations and autonomy organizations. China Statistical Yearbook 2019.

*Table 2.2* Number and types of social organisations in China and selected cities

| | *All Social organizations** | *Beijing*** | *Shanghai*** | *Sichuan*** |
|---|---|---|---|---|
| Social organizations | 366 234 | n.a. | n.a. | n.a. |
| Non-enterprise unit run by NGO | 444 092 | 7148 | 13343 | 24327 |
| Fund organisations | 7034 | 689 | 449 | 1306 |
| Total | 817 360 | 7738 | 13792 | 25933 |

* 2018. Table 1.6 and Table 1.8. National Statistics Yearbook 2019.
** Kang, 2019.Sources:

provinces, while the foundations located there make up 35% of the total number of foundations (See Table 2.2). Foundations are elite institutions, and it is, therefore, natural to find more of them in the richer, urban areas. Sichuan has been a hub for NGO activities since the 2008 earthquake, which explains the large number in the province. At the village level, social enterprise, private business, and social organisation activities are more interwoven due to the multiplex relationships. It is, therefore, likely that social enterprises in the rural areas make up a larger number of the social enterprises.

A recent study, under the auspices of the renowned foundations China Social Enterprise and Impact Investment Forum and Narada Foundation, (www.cseif.cn), sets the number of social enterprises to about 1.75 million units, according to the broad definition.[1] At the other end of the scale are the reported 234 certified social enterprises under a certification scheme initiated by five national institutions: China Charity Fair, Peking University, China Global Philanthropy Institute, Social Enterprise Research Centre, and Narada Foundation. To qualify, the enterprise must have defined social goals, be registered as a corporation or charity with a management hierarchy, full-time employees and income from sales (Yu, 2020). The existence of social enterprises in China is confirmed without doubt, even if their number is uncertain.

## Social innovation policies and the national innovation system in China

China's social innovation policies paved the way for the social enterprises. The policies grew out of the development of China's national innovation system (NIS). An NIS consists of the institutions responsible for innovation policies and processes, like government bodies, R&D centres and enterprises working to develop new technologies that support economic growth (Freeman, 1995; Nelson, 1993). To work well, an NIS needs to be a learning organisation, which requires interactivity and consistent feedback loops between the participating institutions (Lundvall, 2010).

The inclusion of social innovation policy elements in China's NIS has been a gradual, organic learning process. Industrialisation, long the main economic goal, was regarded as the outcome of technology and science innovation. The "National Medium and Long-term Plan for Science and Technology Development, 2006–2020" (MLP) issued by the State Council, and launched at the National Conference on Science and Technology, changed the thinking. The MLP was a fundamental redirection of China's developmental policy, aiming to turn China from a labour-intensive to a knowledge economy (Cao et al., 2006; Gu et al., 2009). An evaluation of innovation management in China ten years after the MLP was launched, found a rapid increase in R&D expenditure, growth in the service sector, the digital economy and the green economy (Gu et al., 2016). MLP's call for the establishment of a national innovation system (Sun & Cao, 2018) and support for indigenous innovation (Baark, 2019) indicated policy changes towards a broader, more inclusive innovation system. In the years following the launch of the MLP, the Ministry of Human Resources and Social Security started to participate in national innovation policy networks and the Ministry of Health and Social Benefits became part of the innovation policy network around the same time (Sun & Cao, 2018). Such changes opened up for social innovation policies.

Innovation is defined as the commercialisation of inventions that results in new processes, products, business models, or markets (Drucker, 2015). In order to qualify as social innovation, the outcome must be improved social conditions. In addition to the social outcome, the innovation must occur through transformative and participatory practices. Transformative practices mean actions and activities with the potential for second-order change; that is, change in the rules that govern those practices (Solov'eva et al., 2018) or systemic social change (Christensen et al., 2006). The rules may be formal laws and ordinances, or informal customs and codes of conduct, which the innovations change. Mere instrumental improvement in the delivery of social services, although crucial in any welfare system, does not qualify as social innovation. Participatory practices mean that the participants in the innovation process have the opportunity to improve their own conditions, as well as to work on the conditions that produced their problems in the first place.

Technological or commercial innovations may lead to systemic social change, but that is not their main purpose. The purpose of social innovation, on the other hand, is precisely to change the conditions that generate social problems – be they due to market or state failure, individual moral shortcomings or physical disadvantages – by including the people who are affected. They are often unable to fashion change because of the way the established system works. The transformative and participative elements of social innovation make it riskier than technological or commercial innovation. Any change in rules can evoke opposition from those who have gained from the system. There is the risk of revolt from those who have not and are free to voice their frustrations and concerns. Careful design and management are necessary to avoid possibly destructive outcomes of social innovation.

The Chinese government solved the dilemma between the need for social change and the need for political control by carefully crafting social innovation into the national innovation system. The broadening and deepening of China's national innovation system was a prerequisite for the emergence of social innovation. In economic reforms, the Chinese government takes small steps and starts with limited pilot programmes. It used the same approach when developing social innovation policies. To some extent, when I used the expression "carefully crafting," it may sound like a systematic process. In reality, the emergence of social innovation, as part of the national innovation system, has been a truly open-ended innovative process.

In the first years of social innovation policies, there was increased emphasis on social management and service systems at the grassroots level, support for entrepreneurship and the creation of problem-solving social enterprises.[2] The latter years, the policies changed direction. The need for increased innovation and labour productivity was met with a combination of deepening market reform and globalisation, combined with the support of state-owned enterprises (SOEs) and a centralised economic programme, as well as re-sinification (the assimilation or spread of Chinese culture) and re-ideologisation of the public sphere (Lomanov, 2020). The raises the question if opportunities for local-level experimentation is reduced. Before addressing the question; it is neccessary to have a look at the effects of the inclusion of the grassroots and private businesses. The first was included through social policy reforms, the latter through market reforms. I discuss each process in turn below.

## Social policy reforms and the growth of the grassroots

While not usually defined as part of social innovation policies, social policies nevertheless shape the opportunities for social enterprises. In China, social policy reforms opened up new opportunities for social organisations of all kinds. In many ways, the reforms have been immensely successful. On the Human Development Index (HDI), which rates countries according to economic and social values, China is the only country to have moved from the low human development category to the high human development category since the United Nations Development Programme (UNDP) first began analysing global HDI trends in 1990.[3] During this period, the average per capita income has grown by 7% annually, poverty rates have decreased significantly, especially rural poverty. Primary school enrollment is nearly 100% and the literacy rate is nearly 97%. Gender equality has increased, the infant mortality rate of 6.8% is low and the maternal mortality rate is rated as very low with 19.6% per 100,000 births. In terms of happiness, China scores in the low middle, number 94 of 150 countries, with 5.12 points of 10 possible. The highest number of points given by the respondents were 7.81 and the lowest 2.57.[4] Such grand average figures can be no more than indicators, but they do indicate that social conditions in China are improving.

Still, there are unresolved social issues. For example, about 85 million people with disabilities still face work life discrimination. The law against discrimination is clear, the practice far behind. On average, this group of people has lower levels of schooling and many families with a member with disabilities have lower than average per capita income. The "floating population" of about 290 million migrant workers live in insecure economic and social conditions, as do many of their "left-behind children" who live in their parents' hometowns with their grandparents or in orphanages. There are about 150 million self-employed business owners, many not managing to pay the 30% of wages in fees to get full social insurance coverage. China also has its fair share of social problems, such as discrimination (Li et al., 2020; Srinivas et al., 2020), drug abuse (Liu, 2015), or domestic violence (Zhang & Zhao, 2018).

Social benefits schemes have been considerably strengthened in the last decades. There are at present five main schemes. Employers cover two of these: Maternity leave and workplace injury insurance. Employees and employers both contribute to the three others: Pension, unemployment insurance, and health insurance. The fees and coverage vary between the provinces but in all 97% of the population is covered by health insurance and about 67% by pension schemes. However, payouts are low, especially in rural areas. In villages, households and families are expected to care for their members themselves. Even in urban areas "the shortage of public services ... has become one of the most important issues of urban governance" (Xiao et al., 2021, p. 5).

There are also some schemes for the benefit of the disabled. Companies have to hire a certain quota of people with disabilities or pay a fee. To deal with the challenges facing the disabled, in 2015 the "Opinions on the Development of Supportive Employment for People with Disabilities" was issued by the China Disabled Persons' Federation (CDPF), together with eight ministries and the National Development and Reform Commission. Local governments were asked to develop supported employment agencies and training facilities. Supported employment involves on-the-job training and involves the disabled as well as their guardians, employers and job coaches who train both employees and employers (Frøyland, 2016). Through supported employment, disabled people are redefined to special-needs workers.

The basis for the policies directed towards specific programmes and groups is China's productivist welfare system. Productivist welfare systems link social policies to economic growth. This type of welfare system was introduced to nuance a commonly used ideal-type typology modelled on the welfare systems found in Western liberal democracies (Esping-Andersen, 1990). The Esping-Andersen typology was used in welfare system research and by global institutions, such as the UN, OECD, and WHO, for policy design as well as to compare social policies globally. Research on welfare systems in East Asian countries found the typology did not reflect basic aspects of those welfare systems and the "productivist"-type was therefore added (Mok, Kühner, & Huang, 2017). In China, the welfare system is driven by economic goals. Investments in human resources are meant to supply the economy with quality labourers and consumers. However, the system is fragmented and underdeveloped (Mok, Kühner, & Yeates, 2017; Qian & Mok, 2016).

Apart from the government, social organisations have carried out many kinds of social work. In the Mao era, social services were "cradle-to-grave" and provided by families, villages or local work units (*danwei*). No social organisations provided services outside the monopoly of the government, which aimed to control all aspects of social life.

In the Deng era, the need for social services changed. Millions migrated from their rural hometowns to the industrialised areas along the coast. Many of the rural migrant labourers did not have the right to social services in their place of work. Social benefits were tied to residency in their hometowns through the *hukou* system. Many children and grandparents were left behind in the migrants' hometowns and were in need of care as well but did not have their adult family members there to provide it. Understaffed and underfunded local schools, health institutions and social services were flooded with new demands. At the same time, SOEs closed down and the urban *danwei* system was phased out. This effectively removed the social services that many had come to depend on. SOE's had provided not only work but also education, health services, housing, social benefits, and pensions to millions who now had to find other means to meet their social needs. Adding to the pressure was the one-child policy from the 1970s that led to a rapidly increasing number of elders dependent on a rapidly decreasing number of younger people. This again meant fewer resources in the families to provide care. In short, the pressure on the existing social services was intense and increasing (Teets, 2012).

Providing social services was not initially part of the market reform policies:

> While pursuing the objective of economic development, societal development was neglected. This is reflected in the reforms of the period (mid-1990s–2003), which overemphasised the establishment of a traditional insurance system, while ignoring the consequences of inadequate insurance in financially underdeveloped areas and among the poor. … Beginning in 1998, the pace of social welfare reform accelerated to meet the demand generated by the market economy (Ji, 2017, p. 99).

The government began to engage social organisations. This way, it could shed part of the burden of providing care by supervising the production of services rather than providing them (Teets & Jagusztyn, 2015). Non-core services were outsourced and new governance mechanisms introduced. The first mechanism was the dual administrative system. Any social organisation wanting to provide a social service had to register both with the Ministry of Civil Affairs and the relevant local-level bureau for the kind of service provided. This resulted in a confusion of routines and huge differences in the quality and form of services across the country depending on the competence and priorities of local governments. Many organisations found it better not to register and instead draw on established local social relations, their *guanxi*. The social organisation saved time and resources on manoeuvring through the convoluted administrative systems, while local officials reduced the risk of having approved projects that did not deliver (Farid, 2019).

As the weaknesses of the dual administrative system became apparent, a contracting system gradually developed reforming the nature of collaboration between the government and social organisations. It started with a few pilots in 2005 and became national legislation in 2013 (Gao & Tyson, 2017). This mechanism is still working. The new mechanism emerged through a few pilot projects both in cities and remote areas (Pan, 2020; Spires et al., 2014; Teets & Jagusztyn, 2015). Chinese social organisations responded with innovative explorations in addressing social issues such as unemployment, environmental protection, pensions, and poverty. Local governments followed suit (Hsu & Hasmath, 2014). As the model spread, a wide range of non-core services were outsourced; for example, legal aid, community affairs, patient outreach, vocational training, food services, and registration of licences. The 2013 legal changes aimed to standardise the contracting system. The expectation was also that by engaging social organisations, participation would increase and lead to closer relations between CCP and the population.

The expectations of the contracting system have not been fully realised. Regulatory complexity has increased, while funding opportunities have been reduced (Kang, 2019), rapidly changing government priorities hamper long-term projects (Gao & Tyson, 2017), and the government's ideological control occasionally backfires (Sorace, 2015). While the climate today is less hostile than it was just after the ban on private initiatives was lifted, the state sector is still weak and relations between government bodies and social organisations are still wary. Diversity is decreasing. In 2017, the new Law on Foreign NGOs has severely limited their opportunities. In total, the expected increase in pluralism and broad participation has not materialised.

A distinct group among the grassroots are the volunteers. Since the Sichuan earthquake in 2008, foreign and domestic NGOs played an increasingly active role in various social projects. The pushes of prospective volunteers and pulls of social organisations in need of hands led to a rapid increase in the number of volunteers. In many countries, a period with volunteer work is advantageous for access to higher education programmes. Volunteering can be a good springboard to launch a career and a chance to get around the world. However, there are also risks to volunteering. It is an ambiguous position in any organization: Neither employee nor customer, neither member nor benefactor. In an innovative move, in 2017, China proclaimed the Voluntary Service Ordinance, giving legal protection to volunteers and establishing standards for good practice. The Covid-19 pandemic has also mobilised millions of volunteers: "According to the Shanxi Provincial Department of Civil Affairs, there are more than 3.13 million volunteers and more than 26,900 volunteer organisations in the province. These people are playing an important role in local epidemic prevention and control."[5]

For social enterprises, volunteers are both a blessing and a curse. They provide idealistic energy, knowledge and plain hard work but they also become competitors. In situations where social enterprises are an unknown entity, they tend to be regarded as providers of a kind of voluntary, free service. As mentioned, this makes it hard for a social enterprise to charge for its services.

## Enter the private sector

The weight of history is heavy on the private sector in China. Merchants were at the bottom rung of the social order in imperial China and their position worsened during the Mao era. The Deng era returned market economy elements to the Chinese political economy. One was the re-introduction of private enterprises, banned almost since the PRC was established.

In a longitudinal study of the emergence of commercial entrepreneurs in China, the authors point to three changes in China's constitution that paved the way for private enterprises (Dai et al., 2019). In 1988, an amendment to the constitution recognised the private sector as supplementary to the socialist economy. In 1992, the private sector was recognised as important to a socialist market economy with Chinese characteristics. Private entrepreneurs were allowed to join the CCP if they qualified through the ordinary application procedures. In 2004, the private sector was to be promoted and protected, not only administered. These changes had immediate results as the number of private enterprises grew rapidly.

Land reforms and the dismantling of small- and medium-sized SOEs resulted in a new type of private enterprise form, the township and village enterprise (TVE). These entrepreneurs were mainly local party cadres and laid-off SOE managers. In 1994 the operations of small business owners, hawkers, street-vendors and "suitcase"-businesspeople were allowed. These microbusinesses have long existed in China, operating at the margins of the economically possible. With the reform, at least their legal protection improved. Finally, in the 2000s, when market mechanisms such as stock exchanges, commercial banks, and commercial law had matured, a new generation of entrepreneurs emerged. These were well-educated people making headway in the telecoms and real estate industries and preferring to keep at arm's length from the political establishment.

In the 2010s, two new patterns emerged. Migrant workers and students returned to their villages to set up new ventures (Wang & Yue, 2015) and the fast-developing mobile and digital economy emerged (Ma & Lee, 2016). The government also initiated a number of administrative reforms focused on downsizing through reorganisation and encouraging government collaboration with the private sector; for example, the 1999 Bidding Law and the 2002 Government Procurement Law (Teets, 2012). Public–private partnership has also been an important mechanism. One example of this is an initiative from 2015. The All-China Federation of Industry and Commerce (ACFIC) and the State Council's poverty relief office launched a programme called "Ten Thousand Companies Help Ten Thousand Villages." Since then, 109,000 companies have joined, creating 199,999 jobs, helping 15.6 million people out of poverty.[6] In line with the productivist discourse, many authors in China define these enterprises as social, because they provide people with a livelihood, especially in the rural areas (Wu et al., 2017). The emergence of private enterprises was crucial for the emergence of social enterprises. Entrepreneurs who had gained experience with business management turned their attention to social problems. Private entrepreneurs have been allies rather than opponents of the state (Chen & Dickson, 2008), but ideological scepticism towards private enterprises is still strong.

Another way the private sector entered the scene was in the Special Economic Zones (SEZs). Here the ideological difficulties were even harder. The first manifestation of the opening-up reforms was the opening of the iconic Guangdong SEZ, colloquially known as Shenzhen after a small village at the site. A large tract of land was reregulated to attract foreign-owned companies to establish production facilities. In 1979 Shenzhen had a few hundred inhabitants. Today more than 30 million people live in the area. Shenzhen is one of the most economically successful regions in China and is known as the Silicon Valley of China.

The decision to allow foreign capitalists access to China was a bold move. Not only did it require massive investments in physical and legal infrastructure, but it also meant dealing with one of the most shameful occurrences in China's foreign policy, the Opium Wars. The Opium Wars were started by the colonial powers to force China to legalise trade in opium, from which the colonial powers and individuals made enormous fortunes. Opium addiction was a severe social problem in China. The losses led China to concede sovereignty to the Western colonial powers and a number of foreign concessions were established. This new construct, the SEZ, evoked old debates about the danger of introducing Western technology and management practices (Simner, 2019). These areas became centres for international trade, over which the Chinese government had scant influence. Another lingering effect of the Opium Wars was a heated debate about importing Western technology. The point of contention was whether the import of Western technology would lead to the importing of Western cultural values and the loss of cultural sovereignty. The issue was political as well as economic, even if it specifically concerned the importing of Western military technology and/or of production technology. Not only was China brutally defeated in the Opium Wars, but it only managed to quell the later Boxer uprising with the help of foreign weapons and had to accept a humiliating defeat against Japan in the first Sino-Japanese war in 1895. In 1914, control over Shandong province, a German concession rich in resources and the birthplace of Confucius, was taken over by the Japanese. In the Versaille treaty of 1919 that ended WWI, after China had supported the efforts with great sacrifice, Western powers broke their promise to return Shandong province. This led to public outrage, as well as the student revolt known as the May Fourth movement, which strengthened the embryonic communist movement. The May Fourth movement again supplied the idioms and symbols for student protest in 1989. "The unequal treaties"-situation ended only in 1941 and to be accepted as equal parties is still an important concern for Chinese business at home and abroad. The story of the Opium Wars has been brought to the forefront again as part of the re-sinification and re-ideologisation of the Xi era. The government has taken command of this discourse, making this history part of the new Marxist-Leninist-Maoist curriculum suffusing all education (Koesel, 2020; Lovell, 2014).

No wonder that opening up for private enterprises was gradual and the SEZs explicitly under the Chinese government's control. The SEZ experiment was successful and has been expanded over the years to International Trade Towns (Belguidoum & Pliez, 2015), e-commerce Taobao villages (Cui et al., 2017), and the less successful Free Trade Zones.[7] These many different projects and initiatives have provided both the government and foreign multinationals with valuable experiences and trained a critical mass of business managers that have turned to social missions. However, the ideological tensions simmer beneath.

As to whether the Xi era will result in the suppression of the unruly energy of the social organisation or private enterprises, it is unlikely the genie can be put back in the bottle. However, the outcome is open. As for social enterprises, it will depend on how they manage their relations with the government.

## Dealing with the polity

All over the world social enterprises operate under conflicting institutional pushes and pulls. The following figure is commonly used to illustrate their typical position at the margins of the market, the state and civil society (Figure 2.1).

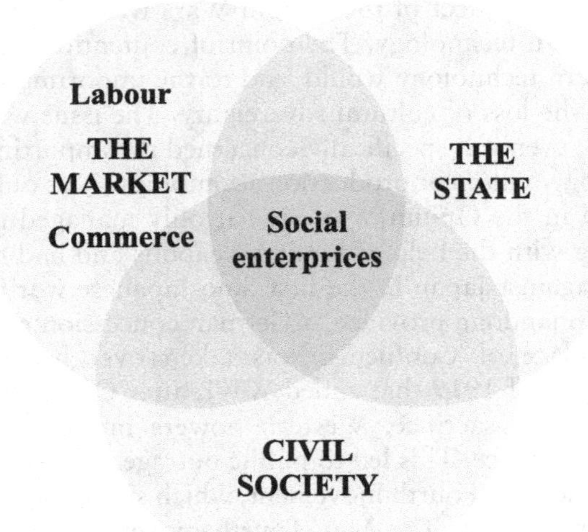


*Figure 2.1* A Westerner's view of the social enterprises in the political economy.

When working on the outline for this book in 2018, I asked a Chinese sociologist if Figure 2.1 could be used to illustrate the institutional set-up in China. Her answer was "if you turn it 90 degrees," meaning the state circle would be at the top (Figure 2.2).

Her answer was a revelation, both about the assumed cultural understanding of the main societal power structures by a Western social scientist and the assumed understanding of the power structure in China by a Chinese social scientist. What was extraordinary was the precision with which she made the cultural translation from one understanding to the other. As the figure is usually drawn, the civil society circle is placed at the bottom, with the market and state circles in line on top. The model is not hierarchical; rather the figure reflects the customary reading of the three circles as interrelated but separate institutional spheres. The challenge for social enterprises is how to balance the conflicting demands between the three spheres. She made me understand that the figure could be read as a depiction of hierarchy too and, in that case, as the CCP constitutes the apex of power, the figure had to be turned to represent that social reality. This social scientist's manner of responding was similar to the way in which others responded. They listened and then used my terms to provide explanations that made sense both in a Chinese and Western cultural framing. This "turn 90 degrees" echoed the "it's complicated" I'd heard earlier. Both are exquisite examples of Chinese statecraft, showing a pragmatic grasp of the political situation in China and the efforts to translate it in culturally acceptable terms to a foreigner.

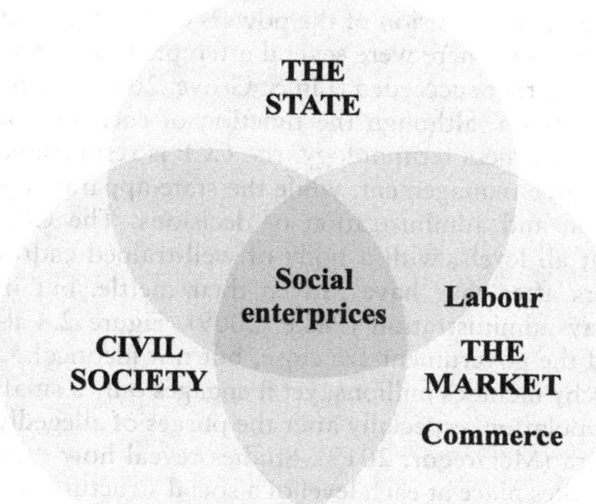


*Figure 2.2* A Chinese' view of the social enterprises in the political economy.

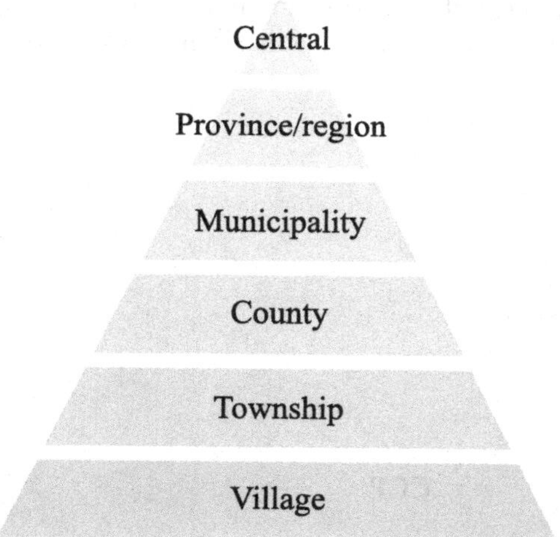


*Figure 2.3* The Chinese polity.

When I started to dig deeper into the literature about social enterprises in China, the hierarchy of the state was better illustrated as a layered pyramid with a small apex and a wide base as in Figure 2.3.

In Figure 2.3, the state apparatus and the CCP are indistinguishable. In practice, this is not quite so, or rather, the relationship has changed over time. During the Mao era, there was a fusion of the powers of the state and the CCP. In the Deng era, however, there were several attempts to separate the powers and, to some extent, that succeeded (Lin & Grove, 2018). In the Xi era, they are being fused again, although the function of each line of command is still separate. In business terminology, the CCP is responsible for strategy and human resource management, while the state apparatus is responsible for the execution and administration of decisions. The CCP provides the government, at all levels, with a body of well-trained cadres that may serve as managers after they have proven their mettle, but in general stay out of everyday administration (Pieke, 2009). Figure 2.4 illustrates how the Party and the government are close, but not identical.

This formal power hierarchy includes millions, yet it engages only a small minority of China's total population, especially after the purges of allegedly corrupt officials in the Xi era (McGregor, 2019). Studies reveal how "the materialisation of ideology takes place at each level of a social structure and players within the economic realm" (Li & Soobaroyen, 2021), and that the national hierarchy of power in China is a mixture of top-down and bottom-up influences, with an immensely complicated, inefficient, and contradictory middle layer (O'Brien & Li, 2006).

The conditions for social enterprises also vary considerably between the provinces, and even within prefectures and regions within the provinces. What will work in a remote village will not work in an industrialised city on the coast. Resources and power are not evenly distributed and economic development programmes differ.

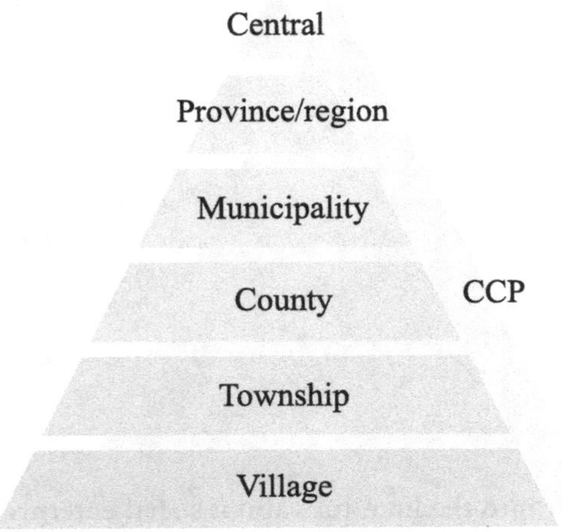


*Figure 2.4* CCP and the Chinese polity.

The egalitarian, as well as the hierarchical, model of the power structure hides one important fact: The weakness of the government and the CCP at the local level. The nature of the political game changes here. Government ends at the village and street level or more precisely, tax-funded regular administrative operations end here. At the local level, citizens must sort out their own affairs through nebulous regulatory bodies. There are party committees or cells at the local level but they do not have the formal power of the bodies within the hierarchy. Furthermore, "the ability of local leaders to prevent conflict and settle disputes is considered an important criterion for promotion within China's local government" (Hillman, 2003, p. 11). Political protests are frequent and accepted as long as they are not directed at the national level or the CCP directly. The situation is different, but equally complex, in what may be called the "muddled middle," every unit between the national and the village/street level. In a study of policy changes in support of social enterprises in Chengdu, the author laconically comments that the requirements of deeper cross-departmental collaborative innovation pose great challenges to the cadres' learning abilities (Pan, 2020). As the local level is where social problems are experienced, this is where the majority of social enterprises can be found. Hence, their space for action is considerable, if they manage their relationships with the government carefully.

Stability is a shared concern at all levels of the power hierarchy and in the everyday life outside it. The prominence of this concern in maintaining the hegemony of the CCP has been a masterstroke of president Xi Jinping (Li & Soobaroyen, 2021), although questions have been raised about whether it is now being supplanted with attention to national security (Fu & Distelhorst, 2020). Its contrast, deep fears of chaos resonate among villagers; senior citizens who remember the civil war; adults who experienced the Cultural Revolution; and the young Chinese whose future prospects are declining in line with their opportunities for education and increases in land and housing prices. While stability, in order to get food on the table, is the main concern at the local level, stability in the population is the concern of the government. What they share is the concern for the stability of China as their home.

## The financial infrastructures

While the regulatory infrastructure of social enterprises is firmly in the hands of the government, semblances of a social financial infrastructure began to appear in the 2010s. This is the result of collaboration between the government, non-governmental organisations, and private businesses.

Compared with big finance and established financial vehicles such as sustainability bonds and IPOs, venture capital funding for start-up social enterprises is limited. The most important sources are the microfinance schemes that have funded rural entrepreneurship projects for many years.

private–public partnerships[8] (Wang & Li, 2019), and, more recently, crowdfunding platforms (Ba et al., 2020; Huang et al., 2018). Other sources are high-net worth individuals (Kang, 2019), and funds from overseas Chinese or grants from foreign charities (Fulda, 2017). For various reasons, foreign sources have dwindled while the interest in social finance from the domestic business community, as well as the government, has increased.

The institutional infrastructure for social finance is being consolidated. In addition to financial capital, it provides incubators and co-working spaces, training, and network access (Sugeno & Yahata, 2016). The institutional infrastructure pools resources from different types of stakeholders and manage the operations through conglomerate-like business models. These collaborative platforms are both domestic and international. For example, in 2016 the Futian district of Shenzhen city announced that it would financially support impact investment (Jia, 2020). With the Xiangmi Lake Consensus in 2017, the China Philanthropy Institute and 77 financial institutions, corporations, educational institutions, and media launched their intention to constitute an impact investment ecosystem (advp.asia/si-landscape). Another example is the China Social Entrepreneur Foundation – the Youchange Organisation established in 2007. In 2017, a number of national-level organisations established the China Alliance of Social Value investment (casvi.org/en). Yet another example is the Leping group, a small organisation with a wide reach in several provinces. The group consists of a foundation, an investment company, a private non-enterprise company, and several limited liability companies. It started microfinance operations in 1993. The Centre for Innovation in Voluntary Action (CIVA), a UK-based charity, organised its first social enterprise project in China in 2013. Results from an action research project were published in 2015, sponsored by the British Council China, the Leping Foundation, the China Philanthropy Research Institute, the Narada Foundation, and the JPMorgan Chase Foundation (CIVA, 2015). More than a dozen colleges and universities have begun to take initiatives such as Venture Cups and incubators or teaching social entrepreneurship.

As in the case of the global social enterprise movement, the movement in China has also experienced cases of fraud that have led to mistrust in social enterprises. This has hit foreign organisations hard (Long, 2016). Social enterprises told me how mistrust required them to be particularly careful to make their accounts public and ensure that all stakeholders were informed.

In the most recent years of the Xi era, there has been a domestic swing in the social enterprise movement in China. The change was initiated by the government but helped by domestic suspicion of the intentions of foreign institutions. This domestic move is apparent in the 2016 "Chinese Charity Law," which simplified fundraising requirements for domestic foundations. However, in 2017 the Foreign NGO Management Law restricted what domestic NGOs could receive in funding from foreign benefactors. In spite of this turn of events, international connections that were important for the emergence of institutional infrastructure continue to be so, as long as they take place within the limits of national policies and communiques.

## E-commerce enabled social innovation and rural entrepreneurship

The mobile economy in China developed faster than in any other country and mobile phones connected the majority of the population to the (Chinese) web in just a few years. By then, Chinese consumers had already learnt that online shopping was safe. This was in no small measure due to the business model of the pioneer digital platforms developed by the now well known corporations Alibaba and Tencent. Alibaba started out as an export broker, providing retailers with a cheap, safe channel to acquire goods from China. Building on its market knowledge, in 2003 Alibaba launched a digital platform, Taobao, intended to facilitate consumer-to-consumer transactions. It rapidly became the preferred retail platform connecting millions of small business owners, entrepreneurs, and consumers. In typical open-source community fashion, anyone could participate if they registered and did not default on their payments or deliveries. Taobao provided a safe payment system, rating services placed checks on fraud and the service fees were negligible. A few years later, Alibaba launched TMall, a platform for professional business-to-consumer sales. The platforms taught Chinese consumers to trust an impersonal system rather than depending on personal relations for their economic dealings (Davison & Ou, 2008). They thus revolutionised e-commerce and facilitated rural entrepreneurship.

Rural entrepreneurship is another fairly recent phenomenon. As mentioned above, the township and village enterprises (TVE) were entrepreneurial start-ups that emerged when the private sector was legalised and the SOEs scaled down. Known as rural entrepreneurship, the growth of businesses in the countryside has continued. The process has accelerated supported by government programmes for rural development and poverty reduction. Migrant workers are either incentivised not to leave, or to return to their hometowns, as are military veterans, to set up new ventures (Wang & Yue, 2015). Likewise, Chinese students who have returned home after finishing their studies, motivated by economic incentives, career prospects or family reasons likewise see opportunities for themselves in establishing their own rural companies: "More than 10 million people have engaged in entrepreneurship and innovation in rural areas so far, serving as an important force supporting the development of the rural e-commerce sector."[9]

Together e-commerce and rural entrepreneurship have generated a peculiar phenomenon – the Taobao villages. That is, villages that have managed to engage a number of villagers in e-commerce, thereby revitalising village life. While this type of venture would not be categorised as a social enterprise in the conventional sense, within the productivist discourse of China, this is a model example of social enterprise. A Taobao village must fulfil certain Taobao requirements: The enterprise must primarily use the Taobao/TMall platform for commercial purposes; annual e-commerce transactions must exceed 10 million RMB (about 12 million Euro or 15 million USD); at least 10% of villagers must be engaged in e-commerce, or more than 100 online shops operated by villagers (Li, 2017). Another study of Taobao villages documents diverse approaches. Qingyan Liu village was the first Taobao village in China. Its business idea was to have villagers rent out empty accommodation for visitors to the nearby Yiwu International Trade City, the largest retail commodity market in the world. The second was Suichang County, where the first county-level online shop for the sale of agricultural produce was established. It greatly facilitated access to the local farmers' market and fair deals, while contributing to stability in the supply of food. The third was Bei Mountain village, where the entrepreneur organised his co-villagers to develop a brand of sportswear, making it possible to increase the prices of the merchandise they already sold, and create demand for better quality (Cui et al., 2017). Although largely concentrated in the south-eastern parts of China, or in proximity to industrial towns or commercial centres, the villages are contributing to a transformation of rural society.

## A Chinese take on two concerns in social entrepreneurship research

There is a large body of research on social entrepreneurship by Chinese scholars. While the domestic research literature refers to the same topics and many of the same theories, it accentuates them slightly differently. There are two unresolved theoretical issues: Altruism and economic growth. As academia is also part of society, the different emphases on these issues in the Chinese literature sheds light on its particularity.

### *Altruism*

As mentioned in the Introduction, the problem of social mission versus profit, or altruism versus self-interest, is debate in the social enterprise field. Social enterprises struggle to balance these contradictory demands and governments have landed on various legislations. Even if it is riskier to be unsocial than commercial, the problem of altruism versus self-interest has also been addressed by Chinese scholars and practitioners.

The unresolved altruism–self-interest dichotomy has plagued economics since its beginnings. Adam Smith, the father of modern economics, in his influential volume *The Wealth of Nations*, argued that an economy depended on human beings' self-interested behaviour (Smith & Skinner, 1982). No artisan bakes or weaves to be kind but to make a living. If everyone behaves rationally, the economic transactions based on peoples' capabilities will match their needs in ways that generate a well-ordered economy. Smith analysed the economic transaction at the time in detail and the theoretical model is precise and logical. The concept of the rational actor has emerged from this foundational volume. It also influences many fields of economics and has found its way into the entrepreneurship and innovation literature. However, the model leaves out a social fact of altruism. Bakers support charity; weavers help neighbours for free. According to the rational actor axiom, that should not happen. The theory cannot account for these empirical facts. A wide variety of theories to account for this dilemma have been proposed. One line of reasoning, from anthropology, is that what is economically rational differs from society to society. Another, popular in economics, is that people are irrational or incompetent in financial matters.

Chinese researchers, however, take their cue from an earlier Adam Smith volume, his *The Theory of Moral Sentiments* (Smith & Hanley, 2010). Far less influential, it is nevertheless more in line with how Adam Smith regarded his own contribution. He was a moral philosopher, not a financier. He, like Durkheim, analysed the societal changes resulting from the economic upheavals of his time, the transition from mercantilist global trade to protectivist national industry. Social entrepreneurship is about moral behaviour, difficult enough on its own, but without adding the difficulty of private economic calculations to the model. This is not to say that economic calculation is not as well developed in China as everywhere else. However, it has not been raised to an end in itself. It is a moral means to the common weal but not a moral end in itself. This reading is in fact more in line with Adam Smith's original perspectives than the later reinterpretation of rational economic actors.

A recent heated exchange between two social enterprise scions in China, the honourable Mr Xu Yongguong and Mr Kang Xiaoguang, demonstrates that it is not only an academic debate. Mr Xu is the initiator and officer of a variety of influential posts in the social sector. He founded the China Youth Development Foundation (Project Hope), the Narada Public Welfare Foundation, and the China Foundation Centre Network, among other influential institutions. In 2017 he published a widely read book *Charity to the Right, Business to the Left*, where he discussed current trends. Mr Kang, a well-known intellectual in the Confucian tradition, takes issue with Mr Xu's perspective and accuses him of supporting economic self-interest, which Mr Xu vehemently denies. When two such influential people engage in public conflict, there are usually more sinister political processes behind the scenes. However, that is not the point here. It is rather the intensity of the debate around altruism versus self-interest and the strength of the altruism argument.

### *Economic growth*

While growth is more broadly defined in the research on social entrepreneurship and innovation, than in mainstream economics, the main thrust is the same – to uncover the mechanisms that sustain economic growth. So also in China, but with a twist. The aim of the research on social entrepreneurship and innovation is to use research findings to develop the economy. The research has an expressed practical goal in line with the productivist welfare approach. An early article from an influential scholar, for example, suggests that the government create a predictable environment for the social enterprises by using the public procurement system or certification and training (Shu, 2010). Another study combines an ideological and a scientific approach and presents a rigorous quantitative study of how close to president Xi's five development goals the province has come (Tan et al., 2020), and yet another extolls the virtue of the goals through descriptions of social impact (Yang, 2020). This emphasis on public usefulness is particular to the academic discourse on economic growth in China.

## Summing up

The social enterprise movement in China is less of a movement than the global one, as it is far too diverse and disorganised to be called a movement: "Still in its infancy, social entrepreneurship, in China's non-profit sector has not evolved into an effective solution to the development hurdles confronting grassroots NGOs" (Yu, 2016, p. 61), and commercial kind of enterprises lack access to venture capital, management skills and training (Jia & Desa, 2020). On the other hand, it is in no immediate danger of repression or obliteration. In recent years, the domestic regulatory and financial supportive infrastructures have matured and strengthened, while foreign connections have been severely restrained. As long as the participants continue to demonstrate how their initiatives benefit Chinese values, they will fit with the ideological re-orientation of the Xi era, as they did with market reorientation in the Deng era.

## Notes

1 cseif.cn/Uploads/file/20190623//5d0f4381b9d97.pdf
2 Xu, Yongguang. 2017. Charity to the Right, Business to the Left. Social enterprises and social impact investing. 公益向右，商业向左. CITIC Publishing House.
3 United Nation Development Programme. Human Development Reports. b http://hdr.undp.org/en/content/latest-human-development-index-ranking.
4 Helliwell, John F., Haifang Huang, Haifang, Wang Shun, Norton, Max. 2020. Chapter 2. Social environment for world happiness. World Happiness Report. https://worldhappiness.report/ed/2020/social-environments-for-world-happiness

5 Yuan, Chengao, March 13, 2020. Millions volunteer to help in fight against virus. http://english.www.gov.cn/news/topnews/202003/13/content_WS5e6aedd2c6d0c201c2cbe3b0.html. Accessed January 18, 2021.

6 Xinhua, September 15, 2020. More than 100,000 Chinese companies help alleviate poverty. http://p.china.org.cn/2020-09/15/content_76704816.htm. Accessed February 14, 2021.

7 Lee, Amanda. August 22, 2019. China's free-trade zones fail to shine despite Beijing's desire to lure global investors. South China Morning Post. https://www.scmp.com/economy/china. Accessed February 14, 2021.

8 Wang, Olivia Yutong and Wo, Bradley. 2019. China social investment landscape. Asian Venture Philanthropy Network (AVPN). https://avpn.asia/markets/china/. Accessed February 12, 2021.

9 Xinhua. January 13, 2021. E-commerce boosts income of Chinese farmers. Xinhuahttp://english.www.gov.cn/statecouncil/ministries/202101/13/content_WS5ffef541c6d0f72576943c9e.html Assessed February 14, 2021.

## References


Ba, Z., Zhao, Y., Zhou, L., & Song, S. (2020). Exploring the donation allocation of online charitable crowdfunding based on topical and spatial analysis: Evidence from the Tencent GongYi. *Information Processing & Management*, *57*(6). https://doi.org/10.1016/j.ipm.2020.102322

Baark, E. (2019). China's indigenous innovation policies. *East Asian Policy*, *11*(02), 5–12. https://doi.org/10.1142/S1793930519000126

Belguidoum, S., & Pliez, O. (2015). Yiwu: The creation of a global market town in China. *Articulo – Journal of Urban Research*,12, 1–39. https://doi.org/10.4000/articulo.2863

Cao, C., Suttmeier, R. P., & Simon, D. F. (2006). China's 15-year science and technology plan. *Physics Today*, *59*(12), 38–43. https://doi.org/10.1063/1.2435680

Chen, J., & Dickson, B. J. (2008). Allies of the state: Democratic support and regime support among China's private entrepreneurs. *The China Quarterly*, *196*(196), 780–804. https://doi.org/10.1017/S0305741008001124

Christensen, C. M., Baumann, H., Ruggles, R., & Sadtler, T. M. (2006). Disruptive innovation for social change. *Harvard Business Review*. https://hbr.org/2006/12/disruptive-innovation-for-social-change.

CIVA. (2015). Social enterprise in China | CIVA. *CIVA*. http://civa.org.uk/programmes/social-enterprise-in-china.

Cui, M., Pan, S. L., Newell, S., & Cui, L. (2017). Strategy, resource orchestration and e-commerce enabled social innovation in rural China. *The Journal of Strategic Information Systems*, *26*(1), 3–21. https://doi.org/10.1016/j.jsis.2016.10.001

Dai, S. P., Wang, Y. Y., & Liu, Y. (2019). The emergence of Chinese entrepreneurs: Social connections and innovation. *Journal of Entrepreneurship in Emerging Economies*, *11*(3), 351–368. https://doi.org/10.1108/jeee-02-2018-0021

Davison, R. M., & Ou, C. X. (2008). Guanxi, knowledge and online intermediaries in China. *Chinese Management Studies*, *2*(4), 281–302. https://doi.org/10.1108/17506140810910935

Drucker, P. F. (Ed.). (2015). *Innovation and entrepreneurship: Practice and principles*. Routledge.

Esping-Andersen, G. (1990). *The three worlds of welfare capitalism*. Princeton University Press.

Farid, M. (2019). Advocacy in action: China's Grassroots NGOs as catalysts for policy innovation. *Studies in Comparative International Development*, *54*(4), 528–549. https://doi.org/10.1007/s12116-019-09292-3

Freeman, C. (1995). The 'National System of Innovation' in historical perspective. *Cambridge Journal of Economics*, *19*(1), 5–24. https://doi.org/10.1093/oxfordjournals.cje.a035309

Frøyland, K. (2016). Applicability of IPS principles to job inclusion of vulnerable youth. *Journal of vocational rehabilitation*, *45*(3), 249–265. https://doi.org/10.3233/JVR-160827

Fu, D., & Distelhorst, G. (2020). Political opportunities for participation and China's leadership Transition, chapter 3 (page 39-83). In. K. J. Koesel, B. J. Valerie, J. C. Weiss(Eds.), *Citizens and the State in Authoritarian Regimes: Comparing China and Russia*. Oxford University Press

Fulda, A. (2017). The contested role of foreign and domestic foundations in the PRC: Policies, positions, paradigms, power. *Journal of the British Association for Chinese Studies*, *7*, 63–99.

Gao, H., & Tyson, A. (2017). Administrative reform and the transfer of authority to social organizations in China. *China Quarterly*, *232*, 1050–1069. https://doi.org/10.1017/s030574101700087x

Gu, S., Lundvall, B.-Å., Liu, J., Malerba, F., & Serger, S. S. (2009). China's system and vision of innovation: An analysis in relation to the strategic adjustment and the medium- to long-term S&T development plan (2006–20). Industry and Innovation, *16*(4–5), 369–388. https://doi.org/10.1080/13662710903053631

Gu, S. L., Serger, S. S., & Lundvall, B. A. (2016). China's innovation system: Ten years on. *Innovation-Management Policy & Practice*, *18*(4), 441–448. https://doi.org/10.1080/14479338.2016.1256215

Hillman, B. (2003). Paradise under construction: Minorities, myths and modernity in Northwest Yunnan. *Asian Ethnicity*, *4*(2), 177–190. https://doi.org/10.1080/14631360301654

Hsu, J. Y. J., & Hasmath, R. (2014). *Isomorphic Pressures, Epistemic Communities and State-NGO Collaboration in China. The China Quarterly*, 220, 936–954.

Huang, Z., Chiu, C. L., Mo, S., & Marjerison, R. (2018). The nature of crowdfunding in China: Initial evidence. *Asia Pacific Journal of Innovation and Entrepreneurship*, *12*(3), 300–322. https://doi.org/10.1108/APJIE-08-2018-0046

Ji, J. (2017). An evaluation of fairness in China's current social welfare system. In Q. Jiang, Q. Lixian, & D. Min (Eds.), *Fair development in China* (pp. 91–106). Springer Science+Business Media.

Jia, X., & Desa, G. (2020). Social entrepreneurship and impact investment in rural–urban transformation: An orientation to systemic social innovation and symposium findings. *Agriculture and Human Values*, *37*(4), 1217–1239. https://doi.org/10.1007/s10460-020-10133-6

Jia, X. P. (2020). Priming the pump of impact entrepreneurship and social finance in China. *Agriculture and Human Values*, *37*, 1293–1311. https://doi.org/10.1007/s10460-020-10130-9

Kang, Y. (2019). What does China's twin-pillared NGO funding game entail? Growing diversity and increasing isomorphism. *VOLUNTAS: International*

*Journal of Voluntary and Nonprofit Organizations*, *30*(3), 499–515. https://doi.org/10.1007/s11266-11018-00085-11261.

Koesel, K. J. (2020). Legitimacy, resilience, and political education in Russia and China: Learning to be loyal. English language version edited by David Hayward Evans, and translated by Manning Ding . In K. J. Koesel, J. B. Valerie& , J. C. Weiss (Eds), *Citizens and the State in Authoritarian Regimes* (pp. 250–278). Oxford University Press.

Li, A. H. F. (2017). E-commerce and Taobao villages: A promise for China's rural development? *China Perspectives*, *2017*(3), 57–62. https://doi.org/10.4000/chinaperspectives.7423

Li, C. Y., Xiong, Y., Sit, H. F., Tang, W. M., Hall, B. J., Muessig, K. E., Wei, C. Y., Bao, H. Y., Wei, S. F., Zhang, D. P., Mi, G. D., Yu, F., & Tucker, J. D. (2020). A men who have sex with men-friendly doctor Finder Hackathon in Guangzhou, China: Development of a mobile health intervention to enhance health care utilization. *JMIR mHealth and uHealth*, *8*(2), Article e16030. https://doi.org/10.2196/16030

Li, X., & Soobaroyen, T. (2021). Accounting, ideological and political work and Chinese multinational operations: A neo-Gramscian perspective. *Critical Perspectives on Accounting*, *74*, 1–25. https://doi.org/10.1016/j.cpa.2020.102160

Lin, J., & Grove, L. (2018). *A century of change in a Chinese village: The crisis of the countryside*. Rowman & LIttlefield.

Liu, Z. (2015). *Current situation of drug abuse and the models of treatment in China*. https://www.issup.net/node/2352

Lomanov, A. V. (2020). Modern China: Internal and external challenges at a new stage of reforms. *Herald of the Russian Academy of Sciences*, *90*(1), 1–8. https://doi.org/10.1134/s1019331620010189

Long, Z. Y. (2016). Managing legitimacy crisis for state-owned non-profit organization: A case study of the Red Cross Society of China [Article]. *Public Relations Review*, *42*(2), 372–374. https://doi.org/10.1016/j.pubrev.2015.09.011

Lovell, J. (Ed.). (2014). *The Opium War: Drugs, dreams and the making of China*. Abrams Press.

Lundvall, B.-Å. (2010). *National systems of innovation: Toward a theory of innovation and interactive learning*. Anthem. https://doi.org/10.7135/UPO9781843318903

Ma, W., & Lee, X. (2016). *China's mobile economy: Opportunities in the largest and fastest information consumption boom*. Wiley.

McGregor, R. (2019). *Xi Jinping: the backlash: A Lowy Institute paper*. Lowy Institute.

Mok, K. H., Kühner, S., & Huang, G. (2017). The productivist construction of selective welfare pragmatism in China. *Social Policy & Administration*, *51*(6), 876–897. https://doi.org/10.1111/spol.12337

Mok, K. H., Kühner, S., & Yeates, N. (2017). Introduction – Managing welfare expectations and social change: Policy responses in Asia. *Social Policy & Administration*, *51*(6), 845–856. https://doi.org/10.1111/spol.12335

Nelson, R. R. (Ed.). (1993). *National innovation systems: A comparative analysis*. Oxford University Press.

O'Brien, K. J., & Li, L. (2006). *Rightful Resistance in Rural China*. Cambridge University Press.

Pan, S. (2020). The development of social enterprises in China. Chengdu city's innovative practice. *Academy of Entrepreneurship Journal*, *26*(2). https://www.

abacademies.org/articles/the-development-of-social-enterprise-in-china-chengdu-city-s-innovative-practice-9164.html

Pieke, F. N. (2009). *The good communist: Elite training and state building in today's China*. Cambridge University Press.

Qian, J., & Mok, K. H. (2016). Dual decentralization and fragmented authoritarianism in governance: Crowding out among social programmes in China. *Public Administration and Development*, *36*(3), 185–197. https://doi.org/10.1002/pad.1760

Shu B. B. (2010). *The rise of social enterprises and development in China*. (Chinese edition). Tianjin People' s Publishing House.

Simner, M. (2019). *The lion and the dragon: Britain's opium wars with China, 1839–1860*. Fonthill Media.

Smith, A., & Hanley, R. P. (Eds.). (2010). *The theory of moral sentiments* (250th anniversary ed.). Penguin Books.

Smith, A., & Skinner, A. S. (1982). *The wealth of nations* (Vol. 1–3). Penguin Books.

Solov'eva, T. S., Popov, A. V., Caro-Gonzalez, A., & Li, H. (2018). Social innovation in Spain, China and Russia: Key aspects of development. *Economic and Social Changes-Facts Trends Forecast*, *11*(2), 52–68. https://doi.org/10.15838/esc.2018.2.56.4

Sorace, C. (2015). The communist party's miracle? The alchemy of turning post-disaster reconstruction into great leap development. *Comparative Politics*, *47*(4), 479–498. https://doi.org/10.5129/001041515816103211

Spires, A. J., Tao, L., & Chan, K.-m. (2014). Societal support for China's Grass-Roots NGOs: Evidence from Yunnan, Guangdong and Beijing. *The China Journal*, *71*, 65–90. https://doi.org/10.1086/674554

Srinivas, M. L., Yang, E. L. J., Shrestha, P., Wu, D., Peeling, R. W., & Tucker, J. D. (2020). Social innovation in diagnostics: Three case studies. *Infectious Diseases of Poverty*, *9*(1), Article 20. https://doi.org/10.1186/s40249-020-0633-6

Sugeno, F., & Yahata, A. (2016). *Study of social entrepreneurship and innovation ecosystems in South East and East Asian Countries: Case study: Leping Group, China | Publications*. Inter-American Development Bank. Retrieved February 12, from https://publications.iadb.org/publications/english/document/Study-of-Social-Entrepreneurship-and-Innovation-Ecosystems-in-South-East-and-East-Asian-Countries-Case-Study-Leping-Group-China.pdf

Sun, Y. T., & Cao, C. (2018). The evolving relations between government agencies of innovation policymaking in emerging economies: A policy network approach and its application to the Chinese case. *Research Policy*, *47*(3), 592–605. https://doi.org/10.1016/j.respol.2018.01.003

Tan, K. G., Zhang, X. Y., & Song, L. (2020). An urban composite development index based on China's five development concepts. *Competitiveness Review*, *30*(2), 137–149. https://doi.org/10.1108/cr-08-2019-0079

Teets, J., & Jagusztyn, M. (2015). The evolution of a collaborative governance model: Social service outsourcing to civil society organizations in China. In R. Hasmath & J. Hsu (Eds.), *NGO governance and management in China* (pp. 69–97). Routledge, Taylor & Francis Group.

Teets, J. C. (2012). Reforming service delivery in China: The emergence of a social innovation model. *Journal of Chinese Political Science*, *17*(1), 15–32. https://doi.org/10.1007/s11366-011-9176-9

Wang, H., & Yue, B. (Eds.). (2015). *Reverse migration in contemporary China. Returnees, Entrepreneurship and the Chinese economy*. Palgrave Macmillian.

Wang, P. J., & Li, F. (2019). China's organization and governance of innovation – A policy foresight perspective. *Technological Forecasting and Social Change*, *146*, 304–319. https://doi.org/10.1016/j.techfore.2019.05.029

Wu, J., Zhuo, S. H., & Wu, Z. F. (2017). National innovation system, social entrepreneurship, and rural economic growth in China. *Technological Forecasting and Social Change*, *121*, 238–250. https://doi.org/10.1016/j.techfore.2016.10.014

Xiao, Z., Liu, T., Chai, Y., & Zhang, M. (2021). Corporate-run society: The practice of the Danwei system in Beijing during the Planned Economy Period. *Sustainability*, *12*(1338). https://doi.org/10.3390/su12041338

Yang, L. (2020). Chapter 4. On the exploration and practice of social construction in Shenzhen in the last 30 years. In Y. Yuan (Ed.), *Studies on China's special economic zones 3*. (pp. 47–57). Springer.

Yu, L. (2020). The emergence of social entrepreneurs in China. *Journal of the International Council for Small Business*, *1*(1), 32–35. https://doi.org/10.1080/26437015.2020.1714359

Yu, X. (2011). Social enterprise in China: Driving forces, development patterns and legal framework. *Social Enterprise Journal*, *7*(1), 9–32. https://doi.org/10.1108/17508611111130130

Yu, X. (2016). Social Entrepreneurship in China's non-profit sector: The case of innovative participation of civil society in post-disaster reconstruction. *China Perspectives*, *2016*(3), 53–61. https://doi.org/10.4000/chinaperspectives.7051

Zhang, H., & Zhao, R. (2018). Empirical research on domestic violence in contemporary China: Continuity and advances. *International Journal of Offender Therapy and Comparative Criminology*, *62*(16), 4879–4887. https://doi.org/10.1177/0306624X18801468

Zhang, W. (2017). The Social Enterprise Movement. In Q. Jiang, L. Qian, & M. Ding (Eds.), *Fair Development in China* (pp. 135–166). Springer International Publishing.

Zhou, W., Zhu, X., Qiu, T., Yuan, R., Chen, J., Chen, T. (2013). English language version edited by Evans, D.H. and translated by Ding, M. (2013). *China Social Enterprise and Impact Investment Report*. English language version edited by David Hayward Evans, and translated by Manning Ding. https://www.ubs.com/global/en/ubs-society/philanthropy/resources//china-social-enterprise-and-investment-report-aug-2013-en.pdf

# Part II

# Cases

# 3 In the international market economy and three case studies

## The dual economy

One result of the market reforms of the Deng era is the re-emergence of two separate economic spheres – a closed, planned one, and an open, market one – in what the Chinese government calls a dual circulation pattern. An economic sphere is defined as the social formation that appears when sets of resources are exchanged between different classes and when the flow of exchanges within each sphere is kept strictly separate (Urry, 1981) This definition is based on Marxist theory but nuances the understanding of the political economy as structured only by socio-economic differences or classes. Classic anthropological studies of economic spheres have documented how people circulate goods according to particular cultural rules and valuations (Malinowski, 2016; Mauss, 2016). Exchanges across spheres are culturally risky, but provide opportunities for making profit (Barth, 2000; Montoya, 2000) Barth 1972 They also provide opportunities for making social change (Barth, 1972). In China, the closed sphere is for Chinese nationals, the open one for foreigners. Strictly regulated economic exchanges between the two are possible, and necessary for foreign social enterprises to make an impact in China.

The domestic, planned economy in China shares many characteristics with "transition economies" elsewhere. Briefly defined, a transition economy is a planned economy that is turning into a market economy by the introduction of capitalist financial vehicles and legal regulations such as credit markets, stock exchanges, commercial law, property rights, and entrepreneurship (McMillan & Woodruff, 2002) that has greatly affected how the economy works. China learns from international business but keeps the domestic and the international spheres strictly apart. At least this is how it is perceived by the international business community. A long-standing business consultant residing in China commented that "The belief by foreign companies that large financial investments, the sharing of expertise and significant technology transfers would lead to an ever-opening Chinese market is being replaced by boardroom banter that win-win in Chinese means China wins twice" (Economy, 2018, p. 142). On the other

DOI: 10.4324/9780429282591-3

hand, the indigenous innovation policies are "in large part a reaction to the fact that foreign companies control virtually all of the technology-related IP (intellectual property)" (Saxenian, 2007, p. 204. parentheses mine). These quotes reflect attempts to make sense of the separation of the international and the domestic spheres. The social enterprise discussed below all operate in the international, market sphere.

## The international market sphere

The international sphere is where the implementation of market mechanisms is most thorough. Although market spheres are institutional and not geographically distinguishable, their clearest presence is in the special economic zones and similar constructs such as high-technology parks, science and technology parks, national innovation demonstration zones, and economic development zones. Zoning off areas to open for trade yet limit contact with foreigners is nothing new, as is apparent from the free trade ports that have dotted the globe for as long as there has been international business (Jayawardena, 1983). The special economic zones are new versions of the free trade ports. The purpose of the zoned areas was to bring jobs and technology to China and to test out market economy mechanisms. China's innovative use of this blueprint for export-oriented industrialisation has made it possible for the authorities to open up the economy for exchanges with foreign companies and countries without losing political control (Wei, 1999; Wei et al., 2020)

Throughout its history, China has swung from openness towards international trade to near-total closure. This has had considerable effect on what foreigners were allowed to do and where. This again has shaped the international market sphere, which has undergone such tremendous changes since 1949 that it is hard to find similarities in the patterns of relations before and after the Mao era. In the Mao era, there were hardly any foreigners left. The Chinese government had total control of the means of production and the flow of people, information and capital. The international market sphere took shape during the Deng era and continued to be refined during the Xi era, which has seen the strongest growth of social enterprises. Still, to understand the situation of social enterprises in this sphere, it is necessary to recapitulate the conditions of the international sphere in the Mao and Deng eras.

### *The situation in the Mao and Deng eras*

When the People's Republic of China was proclaimed in 1949, most foreigners had left China. Those who did remain were either "international comrades," friends or allies of the communists, envoys of other countries, or managers of multinationals (Hooper, 2016). Foreign capitalists found their funds gradually transferred to the Chinese government. Due to the embargo with the USA, supplies dwindled but the government required production to continue and wages to be paid in order to maintain employment levels. Taxes, levies, and other fees soon depleted liquid capital, and the cost of obtaining exit visas depleted private funds.[1]

This was the time of the Cold War in the Western Hemisphere, of which China was on the periphery, firmly positioned within the alliances of communist countries and under the influence of the Soviet Union. Thus, the PRC's foreign trade was mainly with other communist countries. Relations with the Soviet Union were particularly important for the development of China's economy. The USSR provided finance, technology, and training for industrial and military projects. With the end of civil war and heavy investment in new technology, China got back on its feet and gradually became less dependent on support from the Soviet Union. Foreigners were welcome but only as far as they contributed to the country's growth and prosperity as technical experts. Borders were closed, and there were few opportunities for non-Chinese nationals to visit, far less to do business. China's exports were minimal. In 1955, China's estimated foreign trade was USD 420 million with the so-called free world and 2,065 million USD with the communist world. There was even a trade embargo from the USA from 1950 to 1972. All foreign trade with non-communist countries was seaborne, while the majority of trade with communist countries was overland.[2] While China and USA re-established relations in the 1970s, the foreigners did not return to live and work in China until a decade later. In the Deng era, foreigners were again allowed to pursue their economic interests in China, but this time capitalists, in the form of multinational corporations, and later technology start-ups and venture funds, were also invited to participate.

### *The social satellite*

In the international market sphere, there are opportunities for a special type of social enterprise, the "social satellite." Social satellite is a general term for the informally organised activities that emerge in situations where the rules of family life and formal institutions are adapted to each other (Comfort, 2002). Social satellite is also a term used in social accounting, although with a slightly different meaning. A social satellite account provides information about the impact of social measures according to predefined social metrics (Alsamawi et al., 2017). Here, social satellite refers to an enterprise that has a social mission and, for that reason, has separate management and operational routines but in other respects is fully integrated in a corporate hierarchy. Its strategy and management work to realise the social mission, but within the commercial confines of the corporation. A social satellite is a hybrid type of social enterprise with the unique characteristic that it is fully incorporated. The managers of a social satellite are intrapreneurs, entrepreneurs making change from within corporations, only with the exception that social satellites do not only work within the company. Their work, by necessity, also includes engagement with vulnerable groups and the local communities responsible for their care outside of the enterprise, the type of stakeholders as defined by the social mission.

In China, social satellites must bridge the regulatory and cultural boundaries between the domestic and the international spheres. Therefore, the social satellites are good vantage points for gaining insight into the content of the social contract. Because their mission is to solve social problems, they have to be deeply immersed in the domestic sphere where the social problems are. Here, they meet with dominant cultural understandings about disabilities, handicaps, social problems – and foreigners. The managers of social satellites must establish themselves and their companies as trustworthy foreigners, for the transfer of technological knowledge or economic gain. Due to the dual economy, they have limited opportunities to immerse themselves in the local communities to build the required trust. In the domestic sphere, a social satellite must prove its ability to engage in tactful exchanges with families and communities in need, as well as to take care of workers with special needs. They often face discrimination. As a result, many are kept hidden and protected, cared for by relatives who, in turn, are left to bear a considerable psychological and financial burden. Although social satellites in China are deeply involved with families and communities, they are prevented from becoming domestic entities as they are institutionally part of international corporations.

The position of Chinese social enterprises in the international market economy is such that even after the reach of foreign NGO's is being restricted, social enterprises under the wing of foreign multinationals still thrive. This is the setting for Disability Employment Works Ltd. (DEW), a sub-supplier to the manufacturing industry in the international market sphere, discussed below and followed by a comparison with a case from a French business network and another from the United Kingdom.

## Disability Employment Works Ltd. (DEW)

DEW started operations in 2015 as a workshop for people with intellectual and mental disabilities in a multinational corporation in the automotive industry. It is located in Gangshen, an SEZ on the coast of northern China (not the real name of the company or the location). I met one of the DEW social entrepreneurs at an event in Shanghai in 2016, when she excitedly gave a talk about the business start-up. Judging from the responses, what moved the audience most was her tale about the difficulties of gaining the trust necessary to let villagers allow their young adults with disabilities to work for a commercial enterprise. There were two main reasons for the distrust: The shame or bad luck associated with a person with a disability combined with previous experiences of how vulnerable family members had been mistreated by employers. The major part of the evening was devoted to questions relating to these two issues, not the technicalities of starting up a business.

The story behind the start-up was that in 2013, a recently hired European expatriate manager reflected that after his first six months in China, he had hardly seen any people with disabilities. Looking at the people working for his multinational, there were hardly any people with disabilities there either, despite the corporation's explicit implementation of CSR policies and the CEO's reputation for involvement in charitable work. The new manager had previous experience with work life inclusion from the USA and was attuned to the problem. He had also noticed the recurrent frustrations about the unsteady supply of low-tech mechanical parts. These much-needed parts from abroad often arrived at port weeks after schedule or were held up at customs, reducing uptime and productivity at the plant. He combined the two observations and suggested that the corporation set up a separate workshop where special-needs workers would produce mechanical parts. The CEO supported the idea, overruling the initial scepticism among middle managers and local workers. Through his network, he had been involved in a number of earlier local inclusion initiatives started by local business associations and local managers from other companies.

DEW started up in premises provided free of charge by the local chapter of CDPF. A local investment conglomerate provided 50% of the operating expenses for the first three years. The multinational provided machinery and management. Tax deductions and wage support from government programmes provided the rest of the resource base. After three years, it broke even and could cover its own operating expenses from the sale of products. Also, even if low tech, there were high-quality requirements of the products, and DEW met them all.

The first year the factory employed one manager and 12 workers. Three new managers and five workers were hired in 2016. By 2020 DEW had a mixed management group. The majority of managers at DEW are responsible for the conventional functions in market economy companies such as HR, finance, production, and business development. In addition, there are a number of special function managers, job coaches, and a community development manager. With new hires, there will be nearly 40 workers. At first, DEW only served one multinational. Today it supplies other international corporations too. However, it has not been an easy journey.

### *Working with internal stakeholders*

While the CEO of the multinational responded positively to the social entrepreneur's business proposal, other managers, especially mid-level, were not as supportive. They felt the inclusion of a unit with special-needs workers would reduce overall productivity. Some were concerned about their own production quotas, others about the perceived added cost of adjusting machinery and production processes. Such concerns are commonly reported from other countries where supported employment is implemented (Frøyland, 2016). The study also documents a less openly shared manager worry, namely how to behave towards special needs employees.

In DEW, production work was organised in a manner that allowed the employees to gradually learn the required skills, and this was the simplest managerial task. Making the employees understand the need to come on time, be presentable, and speak up required considerable managerial skills like how to give feedback, in particular, negative feedback. The workers were already vulnerable, with experiences ranging from overprotection to abuse. Adjusting production equipment turned out to be less problematic than expected. Training the new special-needs workers took time, but not more than training any new employee. The managers of DEW soon adapted. Changing the mindset of managers not directly involved with the DEW employees was more challenging. Such reconfiguration work is complicated enough in connection with supported employment. Complicating the understanding were different cultural notions about management, work and disability.

Another group of internal stakeholders, the other workers, were as sceptical as the middle managers. They were as concerned with production quotas as with their job security. If people who were perceived to be less capable could do their jobs, it would reduce their social standing as well as their bargaining power. Their fears turned out to be real. While the majority of the DEW workers were engaged in ordinary production, a few were especially adept at identifying low-quality products. When they were promoted to supervisors, also for other production lines, feelings of insecurity and resentment came to the fore among the ordinary workers. They did not want to be supervised by someone they felt was less competent. This occasioned a redefinition of the work tasks and what a model employee is. Carefully explaining that some of the special-needs people also had gifts, the managers of DEW laid the worries to rest by redefining the nature of work and the employees who did it. Unwavering support from top management also helped.

The DEW managers worked hard to change the understanding of work and workers in numerous ways. The major economic change, however, was in the wages of the DEW employees. The DEW managers insisted that the employee did normal work and should be paid normal wages. Companies are incentivised to hire a certain quota of disabled people to get a tax rebate. If they don't do this, they have to pay a fee that is channelled into a fund used to compensate companies for training and support projects. Even so, a large number of companies chose to pay the fee rather than hire people with disabilities. Even more common is to hire disabled people and pay a symbolic wage – to not come to work. This practice means that disabled people are kept out of the workforce, even if the statistics say otherwise.

The DEW managers argued that special-needs workers contributed as well as any other workers, should be paid accordingly and have the same social benefits, including holidays and days off. The workers delivered as promised, the other workers and the managers learnt how to behave in their revised positions, and the customers were satisfied.

### *Working with external stakeholders*

Part of DEWs accomplishment was to change the perception of disability among internal stakeholders. They also managed to change it among external stakeholders such as a network of committed managers from other companies in the area.

Gangshen SEZ, where DEW is located, mirrors the pattern of industrialisation in Shenzhen SEZ. Chinese interests provide the land, plant, and workers, while foreign companies provide equipment, technology, and working capital (Yuan and Lei, 2020). Development of the Gangshen area started in the early 2000s, and it has since continuously been expanded and rezoned in accordance with changing innovation policies. The area was historically a free trade port, and some areas were formerly foreign concessions. The Chinese government invited multinationals from several European and Asian countries, to establish industry in the era and opened up for the joint provision of cultural and educational facilities and health and social services for the expat communities. In 2020, there were about 1,000 multinationals located in Gangshen, the majority European, Korean, and Japanese. A recurrent social issue was the inclusion of people with disabilities into working life. Through DEW, a variety of market economy social practices were transferred to China.

When the social entrepreneur started working with the DEW business idea, the CEO quickly connected him with a network of engaged managers, cadres, and volunteers who had experimented with supported employment. Their initiatives had already generated a special education school, training facilities, and a number of workshop and business start-up projects involving people with special needs. Now the new approach to supported employment was added to the local toolkit and gradually spread to other places. One global multinational with more than a decade's experience with supported employment and training programmes set up a social satellite of its own in 2018. GONGOs, international NGOs, and a number of business associations in China and Europe took note and provided certificates and awards. Demand for start-up assistance flooded the DEW managers, who used it to expand its business and set up a training and consultancy agency. As with DEW, it is expected to eventually manage on its own financially.

The most challenging group of external stakeholders were the villagers. In order to get applicants to the advertised jobs, DEW had to change the mindset of villagers and parents/guardians of disabled people and find a way through the shame and fear connected with disability. Through the collaboration with the CDPF, potential employees were identified, contacted, interviewed, and trained. Only after several years did word spread enough for people to come and ask for employment. This is the situation today, whereas before social entrepreneurs had to travel to villages and neighbourhoods to convince parents to let their handicapped adult children come to work at the plant. The parents had to be convinced that their children would not be maltreated or used as slave labour. Others had to be reassured of their ability to respond to neighbours' fears of malignant forces at work or risks of contagion from a handicapped person. Venturing out in this manner is not an ordinary management task, and through it villagers became a new stakeholder group.

## Other types of social enterprises in the international market sphere

DEW is an example of a typical social satellite. Its position in the political economy is an outcome of a response to both foreign and domestic influences. Although DEW operated in an international environment, it drew heavily on Northern European traditions for supported employment. The other foreign business networks around social enterprises – one French, the other British – are other examples of how social enterprises were established and saupported, in a combination of home country conventions and local conditions in China.

### *The French artisanal tradition*

Shanghai is the third-largest city on the coast right in the middle of China. Its position as a technological entrepreneurship and innovation hub began to blossom from the beginning of the 2000s. Among foreign businesses, it already had a strong reputation for providing foreign companies with efficiency and predictability (Saxenian, 2007). Today it is one of the world's financial centres, housing the influential Shanghai Stock Exchange. The city has always been intensely commercial. It is a transport hub for sea, land, and air, surrounded by high-tech industrial parks and dotted with incubators and work-sharing spaces for start-ups and venture capitalists. As early as the 18th century it was a thriving international entrepôt. Unequal treaties that Shanghai carved up into various foreign concessions in the 19th century are still remembered in the colloquial name of a downtown area called the "French concession." This area has a quaint, artistic feel to it, and today, under special protection by the Shanghai government, it is popular among tourists and expatriates. Known for cafés along plantain-shaded streets, it was a fitting location for a social enterprise specialising in French pastry.

The business idea was hatched by a group of young French adults engaged in the Shanghai French chapter of the Junior Chamber International

(JCI). The JCI is a more than 100-year-old organisation for young progressive changemakers (Lawson, 1996, p. 911). The group of associates had noticed that many international hotels needed qualified bakers and pastry chefs, so why not train locals? So they started the Shanghai Young Bakers (SYB, shanghaiyoungbakers.com). The group partnered with the Children of Madaifu, a charity established in 1999 to help orphaned children, concentrating on Shaanxi, Gansu, and Hubei, a corridor of provinces from the far west to central China. The charity was founded by a French doctor with long experience from Médecins Sans Frontières and knighted in France for his humanitarian work. The Chi Heng Foundation became another partner to strengthen SYB's administrative and management capabilities. This foundation is a Hong Kong–based charity devoted to helping orphans and women affected by HIV/Aids in remote villages.

SYB started its operations in 2009 as a one-year training programme for young, disadvantaged adults and high school dropouts. The first cohort consisted of 16 students from local orphanages who interned at the hotels. For the first three years, two French bakers volunteered to use their spare time at the weekends to train the aspiring artisans. The number of graduates had grown to 30 per year. In 2011, SYB registered as a social enterprise. In 2015 its sister social enterprise, the 127 Village French Bakery & Café, started operations. It was named after the 127 students that had first received funding from the Chi Heng Foundation.

SYB connects with a wide range of external stakeholders in various ways. Volunteers are invited to help in the enterprises or visit villages and orphanages. Founders and managers are involved in workshops where HIV/Aids-affected orphans and women who can no longer do manual work in the villages produce eco-bags. The bag designs express their feelings about their situation. The Accor group in France provided seed money for the workshop and bought thousands of eco-bags for their hotels, where the new chefs were already interning.

The SYB case exemplifies how national networks and traditions both for entrepreneurship and charitable work shape social enterprises in the international market sphere in China. In this case, the social entrepreneurs were far less directly involved with the domestic sphere stakeholders than in the case of DEW. Also, their beneficiaries were extraordinarily marginalised people, orphans, and women affected by HIV-Aids.

### *The United Kingdom charity drive model*

The United Kingdom tradition for stakeholder management generates slightly different conditions for social enterprises. As mentioned, the British Council was one of the early advocates for social entrepreneurship in China. Its aim is to promote British culture and develop cultural relations. As it is a publicly chartered corporation, it is independent of direct government or commercial interests. As early as 2004, the British Council sponsored a Sino-British Social Entrepreneurship Summit in Beijing, gathering British and Chinese entrepreneurs to explore the possibilities for social enterprise development (Zhang, 2017). In 2009 it launched Social Enterprises in the UK, a programme to train, consult, and provide UK social entrepreneurs with resources to scale up their enterprises. In the same year, the Social Enterprise Programme was launched in China and a large group of social entrepreneurs travelled to the UK for training. Before the programme was closed down in 2016, it had supported more than 100 social enterprises in China.

Support for social enterprises has been mobilised from the expatriate community every year since 2011. At the annual ball arranged by the British Council in Shanghai, the community outreach committee elects a number of candidates to receive the proceeds of the conference. The majority of social enterprises supported are engaged in providing health services and education to poor and special needs children in villages in the eastern Anhui, Jiangsu, and Zhejiang Provinces as well as to migrant children in Shanghai. Exceptions to this pattern were Hands-on, a green enterprise for cleaning up Shanghai beaches, and SYB. The latter exemplifies connections between different groups of foreigners in the international market sphere.

## Summing up

The international market sphere is a separate part of China's political economy. For social entrepreneurs, it takes considerable efforts and skills to cross the firm border between this sphere and the far larger domestic economy in culturally and politically legitimate ways. The social enterprises do make a difference, directly in the lives of the employees and beneficiaries and indirectly by raising awareness about respect and dignity for marginalised groups among other stakeholders. In this, they do contribute to changes in the social contract. It remains to be seen if the changes are permanent, or if the boundary between the domestic and the international spheres is too firmly entrenched for the changes to spill over from one to the other. If the boundary weakens, it is a sign that the market economy mechanisms are not merely tools to be applied to improve the workings of the planned economy.

More important for the social enterprises themselves is that their scope for action has not been significantly reduced during the recent more repressive climate. It strengthens the conclusion of those who see that resistance and opposition are possible, if within the system and in order to improve it. The Chinese government shows a great capacity to learn by adapting new and even challenging business models whenever they actually work.

## Notes

1 Wordie, Jason, November 2015. In China post-1949, foreigners paid a price whether they chose to remain or leave. https://www.scmp.com/magazines/post-magazine/article/1875912/china-post-1949-foreigners-paid-price-whether-they-chose). Accessed November 12, 2020.

2 EIC Report on Communist China's Imports and Export. 1956. Trade and Transport involved. CIA-RDP85S00362R000400040001-2. https://www.cia.gov/readingroom/document

## References

Alsamawi, A., McBain, D., Murray, J., Lenzen, M., & Wiebe, K. S. (2017). Review of social accounting methodologies. In A. Alsamawi, D. McBain, J. Murray, M. Lenzen, & K. S. Wiebe (Eds.), *The social footprints of global trade* (pp. 19–25). Springer. https://doi.org/10.1007/978-981-10-4137-2_4

Barth, F. (1972). *The Role of the entrepreneur in social change in Northern Norway*. Universitetsforl.

Barth, F. (2000). Economic spheres in Darfur. In R. Swedberg & F. Barth (Eds.), *Entrepreneurship: The social science view* (pp. 139–159). Oxford University Press.

Comfort, M. L. (2002). 'Papa's House': The prison as domestic and social satellite. *Ethnography*, *3*(4), 467–499. https://doi.org/10.1177/1466138102003004017

Economy, E. (2018). *The third revolution: Xi Jinping and the new Chinese state*. Oxford University Press.

Frøyland, K. (2016). Applicability of IPS principles to job inclusion of vulnerable youth. *Journal of vocational rehabilitation*, *45*(3), 249–265. https://doi.org/10.3233/JVR-160827

Hooper, B. (2016). *Foreigners under Mao: Western lives in China, 1949–1976*. Hong Kong University Press.

Jayawardena, D. L. U. (1983). Free trade zones. *Journal of World Trade*, *17*, 427–444.

Lawson, E. (Ed.). (1996). *Encyclopedia of human rights*. (2nd ed.). Taylor & Francis.

Malinowski, B. (Ed.). (2016). *Argonauts of the Western Pacific: An account of native enterprise and adventure in the archipelagoes of Melanesian New Guinea*. Oxford City Press.

Mauss, M. (2016). *The gift: Expanded edition*. HAU Books.

McMillan, J., & Woodruff, C. (2002). The central role of entrepreneurs in transition economies. *Journal of Economic Perspectives*, *16*(3), 153–170. https://doi.org/10.1257/089533002760278767

Montoya, M. L. D. (2000). Entrepreneurship and culture: The case of Freddy, the Strawberry Man. In R. Swedberg (Ed.), *Entrepreneurship: the social science view* (pp. 332–355). Oxford University Press.

Saxenian, A. (2007). *The new argonauts: Regional advantage in a global economy*. Harvard University Press.

Urry, J. (1981). The spheres of production and circulation. In J. Urry (Ed.), *The anatomy of capitalist societies* (pp. 26–43). Palgrave, London.

Wei, G. (1999). *Special economic zones and the economic transition of China.* World Scientific Publishing Company

Wei, Y. D., Lin, J., & Zhang, L. (2020). E-commerce, Taobao villages and regional development in China. *Geographical Review, 110*(3), 380–405. https://doi.org/10.1111/gere.12367

Yuan, Yand Lei H. (`2020). The poverty reduction Effect of China's special economic zones – case study Shenzhen. In Y. Yuan (Ed)., *Studies on China's Special Economic Zones 3. Research Series on the Chinese Dream and China's Development Path* (1–20). Springer.

Zhang, W. (2017). The social enterprise movement. In Q. Jiang, Q. Lixian, & D. Min (Eds.), *Fair development in China* (pp. 135–166). Springer Science+Business Media.

# 4 The Qushuo Academy – in the modern economy

Most social enterprises in China are started by Chinese people and operate within the confines of the closed, planned economy. Here, innovative, impatient social enterprises must adapt to the slow-moving domestic administrative culture. This has resulted in another unique social enterprise business model. How the founders of one such enterprise balanced government demands and their social mission is the main topic in this chapter. But first, what does it mean to be modern?

In the social sciences, "modern" and "modernity" are used to refer to something new and fashionable or to a specific historical period characterised by secularisation, industrialisation, scientific management, and the rejection of traditions. I use modern here in the latter sense. The Deng era "Opening Up reform" is commonly regarded as the time when modernisation of the Chinese economy started. It certainly was a time when new economic policies were introduced. In the more specific sense of a particular period, however, modernity was introduced in China at the end of the imperial era. Modernity found its specific Chinese form in 1949 with the People's Republic. By the end of the Mao era in 1976, there were hardly any remnants of the imperial bureaucracy that had governed the Chinese state for more than 2000 years. The economically independent business community, as well as the rural and urban capitalist class, were eradicated. The rule of the politically independent village lineages was broken (Lin and Xie, 2018). China had become a truly modern polity; secular and divided into functionalist units geared towards industrialisation. The CCP was in disarray too after the Cultural Revolution but soon re-established its dominance (Koss, 2018). Stability and order returned. However, the imperial governance mechanisms did not. Imperial China is gone. What came instead was a single economic sphere engineered according to Marxist-Leninist-Maoist ideology. It was closed, hence domestic. It was secular, rejected tradition, lauded science and aimed for industrialisation, hence modern. The majority of social enterprises in China operate in this modern economy.

DOI: 10.4324/9780429282591-4

## The Qushuo Academy

The Qushuo Academy (hereafter the Academy) is located in Zisetu County (not the real names), which consists of a small town and a number of small villages strung along a narrow river valley on the coast of Southern China. Its social mission aligns with the government's goal to increase literacy. This has been a policy goal since the establishment of the PRC and China has achieved nearly full literacy among people 15 years and older. In 2019, a total of 96.8% were literate, according to the Human Development Index. However, there is more to literacy than reading and writing skills.

The Academy was formally registered in 2012. Even under the pressure of the increasingly authoritarian government, it has managed to scale up and now has operations in three different locations. Its social mission is to reduce illiteracy by giving children and their caretakers opportunities to read and share thoughts about what they read. The aim is to generate an ecosystem of culturally literate people. While the public school system is tasked with teaching children to read, the Academy aims to make them and their families literate in a broader sense by providing a place where the participants can go and learn to speak up.

The Academy is a thoroughly modern enterprise. It is professionally organised and managed, both according to strict Western business and Chinese Leninist standards. However, there is a remarkable cultural depth to its operations. Its business idea is actually to counteract the negative effects of modernity – alienation and detachment. It also skillfully mobilises historical relationships and idioms in support of its mission, without letting that detract from its social mission. The result is the enterprise makes sense on several levels of meaning. By doing so, it manages to attract resources from a variety of sources, without overstepping the boundaries of any. With the humour, tact, and nerve that characterises much of Chinese activism, the Academy has managed to establish itself as a dependable local social institution.

The Academy is the brainchild of three social entrepreneurs who grew up in the small town. Two of them left to study and then work, one in China and the other abroad. The third remained in his hometown, serving as a Party cadre on projects and committees for many years but had now turned his attention to business. He started a company to manufacture building materials for the construction industry. After only a few years, the company increased its market position to include the whole prefecture and employed several hundred people.

The social entrepreneur living abroad came home to visit and noticed that the town was "dying." There were no art schools, philosophy classes, exhibitions, and shows. The cinema had closed down. Only a public library and a small historical museum were left of the local cultural institutions she had enjoyed in her childhood. The three friends decided to explore possible reasons for the decline. Each had years of business experience, having worked in finance, manufacturing, and real estate. Their initial analysis was like a fact-finding mission for any new venture. They concluded the decline was partly due to the situation in local families, partly to the town's economy. The findings were not in any way unexpected or new but since they themselves had made these conclusions about their hometown, the experiential dimension made the findings real in a manner that aggregate, impersonal studies could not.

The situation in the families was that, as a rule, young adults left the area, as two of the three social entrepreneurs had done a decade earlier. Young adults from poor families in the villages migrated to find work, leaving their children behind with their grandparents. Grandparents were tasked with preparing the children for life in a society very different from the one they themselves grew up in. At home, the children did not have access to books or to adults who could read. The remote parents had to deal carefully with grandparents who had firm opinions on bringing up children. They saw the horizon of their children's worlds becoming narrower than they would have wanted. In more well-to-do families that could afford to support their children with tutors, books, and desks, the children were pushed hard to earn good grades. They had scant opportunity to play or freedom to explore their environment. Eventually they too left to pursue higher education and establish families in their place of work. They returned to visit their older relatives, at least during the New Year celebration.

When I first heard about Zi town at a seminar in Shanghai, it had been described as poor. The first time I visited, I, therefore, expected dirt roads and derelict buildings but it was more like a sleepy suburban centre. There were potholes in the roads, but the bridges across the river were new and safe. There were tired rows of houses along the river, but new rows were built along the lush green hills. The town's economy depended on agriculture and good local produce provided the villagers with a steady income and Zi with taxes and fees. The town was making do, but barely. Its meagre economy was due to poor soil and its remote location. There were no rich overseas patrons, it did not qualify for any of the large government-funded innovation initiatives, and it had little accumulated capital of its own to invest in agriculture or support new ventures. Zi was literally in the middle of nowhere on the horizon of any potential investor. The town officials invested whatever resources were available in upgrading physical infrastructure, not on education or culture.

There was neither supply nor demand for cultural activities. This was the reason why the town was "culturally dying," as one of the social entrepreneurs expressed it. The three friends could have used their considerable business acumen to explore economic opportunities. Instead, they chose to deal with the cultural improvisation and mobilised a large group of stakeholders.

## Why start a social enterprise?

Each of the entrepreneurs who started the Academy had their own motivation for contributing to the project. So did the early adopters, the volunteers who gradually found their way to the project and the parents who sent their children to the Academy. So did the local party officials who observed from a distance, at first, and then included the work of the Academy in their local affairs. As mentioned in the Introduction, Chinese society is defined as collectivist and relational (Yan, 1996). For a social enterprise, it is worse to gain a reputation for being unsocial than for being profit oriented. Social responsibilities override considerations and expressions of individuality and "we" is more important than "I" (Kondo, 2009). However, even in such a collectivist and relational society, people still have a coherent sense of self (Cohen, 2016; Kipnis, 2012).

One of the three founders came from a poor adjacent village. His parents unexpectedly passed away and left him with a younger brother. He had to leave school and find a job in order to make a living for himself and his brother. He had only learnt basic reading and writing skills before he dropped-out of school but taught himself enough to be able to read newspapers and necessary documents. When his brother came of age, this founder became active in the party and started his own business. This extra effort served him well. Objectively speaking, he was doing very well, with a solid income and high social standing in the local community. Nevertheless, he still dreamt of completing his education. When we met, he made sure to demonstrate his reading and writing skills by meticulously writing down what he wanted to say and reading from a little notebook. Only when he had finished doing that would he go on to expand on some particular point. He said he would have liked to have got a degree, preferably in engineering or business, but now accepted it would never happen. So, even if he could not, he could at least make sure others got the opportunity, hence his efforts to establish the Academy.

One of the other three social entrepreneurs, who had coined the term "dying town," knew from her own experience that the public schools taught children to read by rote learning only. She was frustrated that she had never had the chance to think about what they had required her to read. From a middle-class family, she had been pushed very hard by her parents to get good grades and then a proper education. Proper meant law, medicine, or finance. She chose finance, did well and landed a good job abroad. After some years, she came to see life as just a relay race. You were born, studied hard, got a good education, had children. You pushed the children to study hard, get a good education and have children, and so on *ad infinitum*. She could not really see the value of such a life. It was in this mood that she came to realise the lack of cultural arenas and activities on one of her rare visits home. Her depressing sentiments about the meaning of life resonated with her perception of her hometown. In a rapid succession of changes, she found a job in a nearby city, returned to China and began toying with the idea of doing something for her hometown. That something eventually became the Academy.

The parents who brought their children to the Academy did so to support their education. One father was simply looking for good tutors for his two primary school children. They needed more feedback and homework supervision than either the parents or grandparents could provide. Even though the parents were both teachers, and certainly had the competence to tutor their children, they did not have time, at least not in the children's waking hours. The father came across a poster describing the newly opened Academy and finding it met the family's needs perfectly, he became more involved. His motivation was still his children's education, so he contacted their teachers to compare what they learnt at school with what they learnt at the Academy. The public primary school teachers' responses varied. One saw the Academy as a competitor and did not want the extra work of investigating potential synergies. The other became interested and eventually started working there as a volunteer teacher.

The very first volunteer who the entrepreneurs had engaged, had a dream of being a teacher herself. She had reached her goal by a quite circumspect route. Growing up in one of the villages further up the river, she had to walk far to get to school. She loved reading and writing. There were books and paper at school but the teachers did not allow her to take any home. There were no books in her or her neighbours' houses. Paper was expensive and only to be used sparingly. Between her duties on the farm and her schooling, there was little time for what was considered idleness. When she started high school in town, she did her homework in the public library. By then, she had concluded there was no future for her in the village and she was determined to get a higher education. With her meagre resources and limited connections, she did not even consider trying for the national entrance exam to get into a proper college, far less a university. Instead, she applied for a private executive diploma programme in administration in a large city. Working as a clerk and studying in her spare time, she had little opportunity to go home. Only when she was preparing for her final exams did she decide to leave the city for the quiet of her hometown in order to concentrate. She decided to sit in the public library, where there were desks and lights for reading. It was then she discovered the Academy. At first, she could not believe she could go there any time she liked. It was a warm, well-lit place, with desks, books, and the occasional organised chat group – it was unlike any other place she had ever been. After completing her studies, she found employment in the city but she did not forget the Academy. Having more spare time after completing her studies, she went home more often and started to volunteer. She wanted to give something back. Since the Academy had helped someone like her to come up in the world, it could make a difference for other poor village children too. She applied for the position of administrator and became the Academy's first employee, not a teacher proper, but engaged in teaching nevertheless.

As these few glimpses of the stakeholders' various motivations show, they were based on personal experiences and needs. These private, idealistic, and existential drives fueled the start-up. In order to get a business running, however, that kind of energy is not enough. When the founders had found the why, the question of how still remained.

## How to start a social enterprise?

The founders started with the understanding that their hometown was culturally impoverished and wanted to change the situation, but finding out precisely what to do took time. Again, they used their business experience. They needed a vision, a beacon to guide them. Culture can be enhanced in many different ways. What the founders finally agreed on was reading and writing skills. They could start an educational institution in support of literacy. Not only was this in accordance with government priorities, but it was also a logical conclusion to their assessment of the situation of the dying town. If more children became literate, they could gain access to the views of the wider world without having to leave town. They would become more creative, more outgoing and could contribute to the growth of the town, be it as businesspeople or artists. It would also increase their identification with their hometown, not only as a place where their parents and grandparents lived but also as a place for belonging to a family and being a cultured, Chinese person. The concept of literacy was a simple formula, easy to communicate, yet it had deep symbolic meaning.

Even if the vision of literacy is general, it also helped the founders to focus. They decided not to do anything that did not support reading and writing. In their pragmatic, business approach, the founders explored what reading and writing meant, technically speaking. Knowledge of Chinese characters was obvious, and so was having access to books to read and paper to write on. They considered a range of other practical matters such as where to meet, the need for equipment, how to attract users and what kind of users, how to fund activities. This process took a couple of years. It required meticulous intellectual work and hard prioritisation to discover the most viable way to turn a vision into a social mission. The first activities organised by the Academy were simple reading sessions for children run by parents and volunteer teachers.

## The management structure of the Academy

The Academy was registered as a non-profit social organisation. The founders found the risks too high with a commercial venture. Engaging in commercial transactions would give them a different position in the local economy and make the enterprise vulnerable to solicitation and corruption. The Academy was thus economically dependent on donations and grants. The three founders and their families provided the start-up capital and, in the beginning, they made up the decision-making body of the Academy, the council. However, they carefully avoided the position of owners. Instead, other stakeholders, volunteers, parents, and teachers were fully engaged in the deliberative decision-making processses. The process was modelled neither on the conventional total management control common in business, nor the consultative approach common in the Chinese polity, but on the deliberative practices of voluntary associations. The council members filled the position of representatives. They represented the social mission, both externally for government officials and parents, and internally for the volunteers.

All activities were project-based for the first four years. The founders set up an agile organisation in order to maximise learning and training. At first, they depended on their own ideas, but after having mobilised a number of volunteers they were included in the idea-generating process. Interestingly, this set-up resonates equally well with the ideas about good governance common in a freedom-oriented entrepreneurship community and those in a control-oriented Leninist Chinese government. In the Academy, whenever someone had an idea for an activity, he or she was required to share it with the others in a meeting. A decision to follow up or not would then be made after due deliberation within the whole group. Only after such a seemingly slow-moving process would an activity be started. A designated group of volunteers would find resources, plan and execute the agreed activity. Several activities were initiated, like a reading circle, an evening class, and experiments with new pedagogical methods. Many only happened once. The activities that did continue would be vetted after a few months. The council and the core group of volunteers would make an assessment and give feedback on how people were doing. As they were well-versed in the Maoist-Leninist routines of self-criticism, the feedback would be succinct, direct, and public. Also, the demand from the market, parents, and children had to be documented, in accordance with Western business practices. If the general agreement was that the activities contributed to the Academy's social mission, a prioritised project would be defined and get its share of the donations and access to equipment and rooms. The groups that had successfully started could then initiate new activities or merely continue to run the project. In this manner, the Academy developed organically through processes of wide consultation among people who had proved their mettle and with activities that were in demand.

Soon enough resources were committed so that the Academy could hire its first employee. In 2012, the formal management structure of the Academy consisted of the council and one employee. By 2016, there was seven staff members and about 1,000 volunteers, including summer interns from foreign colleges. In 2018, a franchise was initiated in an inland town, and another was planned in 2020. Strategic decisions are now made in a central council of three businesspeople, one academic, one employee, and one social activist, while local committees and managers are responsible for each of the local academies, their employees, volunteers, and beneficiaries.

The range of activities has expanded considerably. While in 2012, the focus was on students' reading skills, later the participants included groups of adults, women, teachers, graduates, and parents with a craving to increase their own learning. While classes for children were the main activity of the Academy, adult reading and reflection groups became another mainstay. After two years, the Academy decided to open mobile school units in the villages as they found that village children and their caretakers did not have the opportunities to travel to town for classes. The next activity was hosting cultural events. Six years after its registration, the Academy had hosted about 750 public activities, reaching in all around 40,000 participants.

The Academy regularly publishes its accounts on its home page, providing detailed information about income and expenditure, the names of donors and the amounts granted. Even today, the enterprise is funded solely by donations, in money and in kind. All books and furniture, buildings, and equipment are donated. Around 20% to 30% of the money comes from government sources, 50% from volunteers and readers, and the founders and their families still cover the gap between income and expenses. The ambition is to make the Academy entirely independent of the economic support of the founders.

## The social impact

The Academy made a point of measuring its social impact and publishing these results regularly. This also helps it to solicit donations. Its direct social impact was improved reading skills among the students. As the activities are classes for children and youth, reading and discussion events, and simply providing a place for people to study, the Academy contributes to increase literacy rates. It also extends its reach through the mobile schools in the villages. One in seven of the households in the town has accessed the Academy.

The indirect social impact is that volunteers and users learnt to professionally operate an organisation and how to make changes. Another is the revitalisation of cultural institutions. So, in different ways, the academy creates ripple effects within the town. The direct economic impact is job creation. The indirect economic impact is on the (local) culture industry, an example being the reopening of the local cinema.

The Academy has also added to a sense of local cultural identity, although this is rarely brought out in the open. The first time this was evident was when, during a brief conversation I was witness to during a lunch, one of the employees apologised for excluding several of those present by speaking Wu among themselves about some urgent administrative matter. She explained that Wu was an ethnic minority language. Confused, I said I thought they were all locals. To my amusement, they explained that although Han Chinese, they were also descended from the Wu state, which had ruled the area some hundred years earlier. People in the area still retained a number of local customs, and the local museum displayed artefacts found in the valley from the Wu dynasty. Archaeological digs had even excavated implements and tools dating back to prehistoric times. The remembrance of this historical legacy gave additional depth to the Academy's social mission. Revitalising a dying town was not only a way to improve the quality of life of the living but also a way to honour the accomplishments of previous generations.

## Government involvement

Council members take care to discuss their plans with government officials and to include Party cadres in their deliberations. If the government asks them to do things that are against their vision, they will say an outright no to even minor things, such as banners outside the building for a delegation visit. For larger issues they "will find a way to say no." For example, while the academy has avoided being seen as a competitor of the local schools, there is competition with the local public library. In the view of the volunteers, the government allows private social initiatives in order to create competition with their own institutions. Successful new ventures are co-opted and included in local government activities.

Before 2012, the Academy ran activities in whatever rooms the founders and volunteers managed to borrow and with whatever material they could get. Even if the first year was a bumpy ride, enough activity went on to give the founders a sense of being on the right track. Then the grandmother of one of the volunteers suggested that an old derelict building on the outskirts of the town could be used as a permanent site for the Academy. The building was located in a former industrial site with four other large halls around a small courtyard. It was accessible through a single main gate. The site had been abandoned for several decades. The buildings were in bad repair and the little yard was overgrown with weeds. However, it was easily accessible from all parts of town, with parking space and lots of rooms. Now came the more delicate matter of getting permission from the town government to use the building. That also meant drawing attention to the activities of the Academy, which thus far only had been more like a group of friends and acquaintances helping children with their homework than an actual organisation. The Academy had not attracted much interest from the government, anyway. It was a bottom-up development project at the muddy interstice between the village and township level, too far from county and prefecture political processes to warrant attention and resources.

The question of using the old building changed the situation. First, it brought old wounds to the surface. The land had belonged to the grandmother's lineage for hundreds of years. Her grandfather had managed to get a little piece zoned to an industrial site in the 1920s. At that time, the national industries of the Chinese economy were still growing (Zhang, 1992). During the Mao era, in the collectivisation of the 1950s, the lineage's property was all taken over by the CCP. The industrial site was used for the collective storage of rice and other produce. After the collectivisation period, the site had been used for various other government projects until it was closed down for being too worn down and outdated. However, all the while, the grandmother's lineage had maintained ownership of one of the five buildings, or so they claimed. One of the volunteers mentioned this on a visit to the site. To me this was surprising, as I believed that private property rights had been abolished in the Mao era. I never got the full story, however. When I later asked her, the grandmother just shivered, mentioning "the dark years," and her visible discomfort had us all quickly turning to another topic. The other Academy people were uncertain about the details.

By suggesting the use of the building, the grandmother had actualised the position of the owner of the property. This was legally and ideologically problematic, but historically correct. The grandmother's claim was acknowledged in a kind of tacitly agreed usury right to the building and the Academy opened there under her protection. The change of purpose for use of the building required formal government approval. The founder, who had been an active cadre before he turned to business still had an extensive network in the local government and he facilitated the application. He and another of the founders, who had long experience in the construction industry, checked the safety of the building and made sure to get all the required documents in order.

When the formalities were in order, volunteers and business contacts helped refurbish the building and equip it for school use. They partitioned the walls to make several smaller rooms and painted corridors with brightly coloured flowers at child height. The entrepreneurs begged and borrowed desks and chairs from companies going out of business, kindergartens, and schools. They also started to collect books. At first, the founders concentrated on getting children's books. Street markets in the large cities in China are overflowing with used books and the word was sent out on social media. Soon a steady flow of books came from visitors. From how the pioneers described it, the first four years were blissful. The building was full of children, reading, playing, and talking. Parents gathered for discussion groups relating to education. In the declining economy of the town, a number of unemployed adults, homemakers, and grandparents also began to see the benefits of volunteering. The founder's idea to enliven the town had started to bear fruit.

Then, in 2015, the town officials and Academy founders agreed to set up a new building on a small piece of land by the river, closer to the town hall. Several of the volunteers longed to be back in the old site, but all agreed that the Academy had no choice but to comply with the Party's wishes. The plot of land had been zoned for industry but turned out to be too small to be of interest to investors or entrepreneurs. Fully prepared with technical infrastructure, it had lain empty for some years. Now it was overgrown with wild grass and weeds, much like the old Academy site, but with beautiful old willows on a riverbank, a perfect spot for reflection. The Party committee and township administration wanted something done with the idle tract of land. The two shared a multi-storey steel-and-concrete office building a few minutes drive from the vacant plot. After careful consideration and negotiations, the Academy agreed to the proposal but took control of the design and construction of the new building. It opened in 2016. The building, a concrete and steel functionalist design, has two storeys; with classrooms on the ground floor, and meeting rooms and a library on the upper floor. Its glass exterior mirrors the willows and the river and on sunny days it looks like a gem in the greenery. One of the upper rooms is jokingly referred to as the "propaganda room" because, as part of the deal, the government can use it freely whenever it needs a private meeting room. It is also the room where tea ceremonies are held, and where foreigners are introduced to the Academy. On the other side of the stairs is the library, the pride of the council and the volunteers. It was completely furnished through donations and the names of these donors are on plaques on the bookshelves and desks. The books were also donations, and the library had an impressive and varied collection. On an upper shelf, about ten metres of books in gold binding are half-hidden by the eaves of the shelf. These are the full range of Buddhist teachings donated by a Party official, as a tribute to his hometown explained one of the volunteers.

## Resisting government co-option

The donation of Buddhist scriptures from a cadre in the explicitly atheist CCP revealed the rich complexities that the young writer referred to when I asked about the role of the party for social enterprise in China. On the bookshelves of the Academy was an example of how complexities were worked out . The story of how an Academy managed to say no to a request of strategic importance to the local government is another example.

On one of the hills along the river is an old pagoda-like structure. I had asked about it several times. It looked like a small temple or watchtower, but no one could explain what it was. Then one day the volunteers took me hiking. The hike was steep, through jungle-like greenery that limited the view completely. The vista that opened up after about an hour's climb, however, was spectacular. In the far west, we could see the entrance to the valley, with the road and railway line. Dotted along the banks were the villages. The river meandered down past us and continued around a bend to the east. Down on the south side of the hill were other settlements, not directly accessible from this valley as far as I could see. To the north was the town itself, laid out in irregular plots, small stores, and workshops mixed with residential areas. The highest building was the town hall. Further downriver, by the willows, the academy glittered in the sun.

The volunteers had taken me straight the pagoda-like structure that had piqued my curiosity. It was solidly built. Wooden boards with poetry in beautiful blue calligraphy adorned each of the four doors of the octagonal building. The doors were locked, but it was possible to peek through cracks in the boarded-up windows. There was a large main hall with stairs leading to the second-floor open balcony. At the back was a partition wall with some cleaning equipment. The hall was sombre, silent, and very dusty. To the south of the pagoda were a few outhouses. It turned out that the local government had refurbished it some years back, intending it as a place for quiet literary study. It was a pavilion for academics and artists but had attracted neither scholars nor poets. No wonder, I thought, with such a steep climb and no place to stay overnight. The town authorities had then approached the Academy and asked them to take over management of the building to arrange poetry sessions, literary events, and seminars. The academy firmly declined the request with reference to its social mission to strengthen literacy. Managing a retreat for scholars was way outside its mission. It took some careful interaction to get the government to accept its stance but eventually, the requests stopped.

Another surprise was that in the valley to the south shone a bright, large building. It turned out to be the newly renovated lineage temple for people sharing one of the dominant surnames in the area. It is a much larger complex than the scholar's pavilion and includes education and health facilities that the local community welcome. A wealthy overseas Chinese man paid for the renovation as a tribute to the land of his ancestors. The fact that the lineage had been eradicated and gone for many years was not of much concern to the locals.

As if to balance stories about traditional superstitious beliefs, one of the volunteers pointed to another hill and said that, according to her grandfather, the People's Liberation Army (PLA) had appeared from that direction. The valley was among the first areas to be liberated by the PLA. Because the area was so poor, the communists had long had strong underground support from the townspeople and villagers. They happily welcomed the soldiers after the long years of civil war and the Japanese occupation of nearby areas.

## Experiencing the complexity

My interest in the Academy started when I was looking for case studies from China to use in my teaching. Only later did I find out how much of a hassle my visits were for the Academy. It added to my understanding of the complexities the young writer mentioned at the start of this book had tried to explain.

The first time I visited the town, my hosts provided me with a travel companion on the train from Shanghai. They told me he was a schoolmate of one of the founders. It had turned out that we were going to visit on the same day and, therefore, might as well travel together. At the train station he was not at the assigned meeting place and, after waiting as long as practically possible, I finally had to board the train alone. I sent him a message asking if he was okay, secretly relieved that I could relax on my own on the several-hour-long train ride. To my surprise, he answered that he was on the train. In case his true mission was to keep an eye on me, I made sure to let him know my seat number and invited him over for a chat. He said, yes, he would come, only there was this and that he had to do first. We exchanged messages for the rest of the train ride.

An Academy volunteer was waiting at the train station, where I finally met my "travel companion." We drove straight to a restaurant where four others were waiting in a *chambre séparée,* among them one of the Academy founders I had met previously in Shanghai. The others were strangers. Managing in a mix of English and Chinese, the conversation soon flowed.

The founder and my travel companion teased each other continuously. Others shared their stories and were curious about me. It was great fun. Then something strange happened. My travel companion suddenly excused himself and left the table to go to the washroom. On the way, he grabbed his mobile phone. As he locked the door behind him, the founder shouted to him and jokingly accused him of being a spy who was going to report on us. The guy quickly opened the door and came towards us. Red-faced he banged his phone on the table and returned to the washroom. Nothing more was said about this after he came back but the lunch ended soon after. The scene strengthened my assumptions of why he had come. I interpreted the incident as a message to all from our host to be careful about what we said. In Shanghai it was rumoured that a foreign social entrepreneur had gone into hiding after the homeless shelter he ran had been raided. Word was out that social entrepreneurship could be regarded as a kind of social activism. It was best to be careful.

After my second visit to the town, my host explained that, in order to prepare, he had to send a note to the local government with the purpose of, and programme for, the visit. Afterwards he had to send a report detailing what had happened. The first two visits were easy to report on. They consisted of meetings at the Academy and visits to restaurants for lunch. I asked if it was too much of a bother, but it seemed to be okay. I was eager to follow the progress of the Academy, to learn how to grow an actual social enterprise in China. Also, I loved the visits to the tranquil town, so different from the intense megacity where I lived. The locals insisted that the town did not have any tourist appeal, a point of view that I did not share and the visits certainly did not expel my fascination.

One day, the grandmother who donated the building to the Academy invited us to lunch at her house. Located in a new part of town, the house was a semi-detached with a beautifully groomed front porch. She had made one of my favourite desserts and I could hardly wait. The door to the porch was open and, while we were eating, a man suddenly walked in. He appeared as a typical senior government official, with black hair, impeccable sharp black trousers and a white shirt. He exuded the kind of pent-up aggressive energy I had come to associate with prominent Party officials and commanded the room the minute he walked in. The grandmother smilingly introduced us. He turned out to be a neighbour and the local Party secretary. He was just popping in as he walked by, or so they said. All sat down again and a halting conversation began around the table. The Party secretary spoke mostly with the grandmother. It turned out they were childhood friends. He sent a question or two in my direction but, apart from that, we did not interact. The Party secretary quickly finished his lunch, we exchanged symbolic gifts and he left.

On subsequent visits to the town, I was allowed to walk along the river and into the hills with some of the volunteers, meet with parents and foreign volunteers and even have lunch with a recently decommissioned young soldier who had started working as a volunteer. He was handicapped too, so one of his tasks was to figure out how to make the Academy better fit for people with disabilities. It turned out he was interested in Scandinavia. Obviously a nerdy guy, he nevertheless, to my astonishment, knew historical details that I would not have expected even the average young Norwegian to know. Even if I suspected that he had been instructed to learn a few details by heart to be a good host, I was moved to be trusted with a vulnerable youth. I was also aware of being drawn into social interdependencies that I hardly understood. My intention in visiting the Academy was to check if it was a *bona fide* case. Then the rapidly growing social enterprise intrigued me. Grateful for their hospitality, I had offered to contribute as a volunteer but had been politely refused. Now, I finally felt useful. I was an opportunity for the young volunteer to interact with a foreigner. In this way, and in many others, I began to be drawn deeper into the complex tapestry of Chinese society. Gradually, the full implications of the young writer's comment that "it's complicated" to engage in social entrepreneurship in China came to life.

## International connections

There were other foreigners far more engaged in the Academy than me. The founder who had worked abroad had connections with universities and colleges in Canada and the USA. She had managed to get the academy qualified for several exchange programmes for volunteers. I met a couple of them. One shared his experiences on social media. He described how during teaching a course he noticed the students were shy and did not express themselves. They were unused to classroom activities not directly related to grading. After steadily encouraging students to share their ideas rather than search for the right answer, he noticed how they eventually warmed to the new pedagogical approach and became more vocal and expressive.

The founders also had connections with wider social enterprise movements. They held positions in the governing bodies of other social enterprises and advised foreigners who attempted to set up social enterprises of their own. One of the other enterprises was a national, private foundation, which funded its activities from charity drives. This business model was similar to the UK approach discussed in Chapter 3, except the main benefactors were youth from wealthy Chinese and international families. The founders also had connections with the global movement and were well-versed in the international literature on social entrepreneurship. However, direct contact with foreigners was limited to volunteers and *ad hoc* visitors like me. No foreign institutions provided the Academy with funds or training. While the founders had strong global connections, their enterprise was fully immersed in the domestic, modern sphere.

## Summing up

Social enterprises have a more direct impact on the social contract in the domestic sphere than in the international one. As the Academy case demonstrates, its operation has a direct impact on the beneficiaries, but also has a wider indirect impact. It succeeded in revitalising the cultural life of the town.

All stakeholders carefully interacted in ways that made it possible to sort out potential conflicts and resistance, without causing public loss of face or reputation. Professional management tools that the founders had learnt abroad had been introduced not only in the enterprise but also to other stakeholders. Ownership rights from the time China had been deeply involved in international trade had been revitalised through access to the old industrial building.

## References


Cohen, A. P. (2016). *Self consciousness: An alternative anthropology of identity.* Routledge.

Kipnis, A. B. (Ed.). (2012). *Producing Guanxi: Sentiment, self, and subculture in a North China village.* Duke University Press.

Kondo, D. K. (Ed.). (2009). *Crafting selves: Power, gender, and discourses of identity in a Japanese workplace.* University of Chicago Press. https://doi.org/978-0-226-09815-9.

Koss, D. (2018). *Where the party rules: The rank and file of China's communist state.* Cambridge University Press.

Lin, Y & Xie, Y. (2018). *Century of change in a Chinese village: The crisis of the countryside.* Translated and edited by Linda Grove. Rowman & Littlefield.

Yan, Y. (1996). *The flow of gifts. Reciprocity and exchange in a Chinese village.* Stanford University.

Zhang Z. (1992). The development of Chinese national capital in the 1920s. In T. Wright (Ed.) *The Chinese economy in the early twentieth century. Studies on the Chinese economy* (pp. 44– 57). Palgrave Macmillan, London.

# 5 The Baisha Naxi Embroidery Institute in the moral economy

A number of social enterprises in China are started by China's ethnic minorities. These enterprises operate within an economic sphere of their own, the moral economy, governed as much by ethnic custom as global and domestic influences. The social enterprise business model that appears from this context is again different from those introduced in previous chapters. Ethnic minorities are a politically sensitive issue in China. Being an ethnic minority social enterprise, therefore, adds another layer of complexity to the story of social enterprises in China.

## The moral economy

The term "moral economy" refers to pre-modern economies based on custom and mores, not law, science and technology (Adelman, 2020; Götz, 2015). Adam Smith, for example, takes pre-industrial social life for granted even as he tries to develop an analytical framework for analysing the emergent modern economy (Thompson, 1971). Emile Durkheim, a century later, critical of political economic theory and deeply worried about an apparent lack of morality, investigated the disappearance of the moral economy (Wilson & Dixon, 2014). The division of society into economic sectors only came with modernity. With the nation state, industry, and work life as the dominant public communal arenas, moral communities were relegated to the margins of society in practice, as well as in academic theories and ideologies. Despite the many groups who continued moral economies, there was little interest in the economics of stateless, so-called primitive societies, apart from within a few academic fields, such as anthropology and sub-fields of economics. The empirical reality of moral economies was hardly conceptualised in mainstream social science. However, the concept of the moral economy has come to the fore again also in studies of the position of marginalised groups in industrial, market economies. Examples include peasant communities in rural Burma, Vietnam, and China (O'Brien & Li, 2006; Scott, 1976), Chinese family businesses in urban Malaysia (Brøgger, 1989; Hallgren, 1986) and Arab merchants in the city state of Singapore (Manger, 2013). The meaning of

DOI: 10.4324/9780429282591-5

the concept is clear, whether it is applied to a rural, subsistence economy or an urban trade-based one. A moral economy is composed of exchanges regulated by customs and shared cultural standards among a group of people, regardless of their political legitimacy or economic situation.

## The ethnic minorities in China

There are 56 publicly recognised ethnic minority groups in China, estimated to be about 100 million people.[1] The ethnic minority definition is a historical construct. During the republican era, all ethnic groups were regarded as belonging to one Chinese nation and ethnic differences were regarded as politically irrelevant. That changed in the Mao era. Systematic research was done among a number of ethnic groups in order to ascertain if they were indeed culturally separate. A number were then recognised and placed under the appropriate government administrative unit. This meant that the unique cultural heritage of at least some groups was acknowledged (Hillman, 2003; Zhu et al., 2017). Other groups were lumped together under the same ethnic category and found themselves governed by the same official unit. In many cases, ethnic groups, such as the Wu mentioned in chapter 4, were simply defined as Han Chinese, and appear as such in the public registries, while dialects and local customs were maintained (Dikötter, 1997).

A dominant idea during the Mao era was that the non-Han ethnic groups were locked into older, exploitative economic relations and therefore in need of liberation. The liberation followed the cultural conventions of the Han Chinese. Many years ago, a Chinese scholar explained to me that it had been scientifically proven that the evolution of humankind proceeded through various economic stages. We were discussing anthropology and he was explaining his theory of science, using the ethnic minorities in China as empirical examples. He said that the ethnic minorities were poor and their economies underdeveloped. Therefore, it was the moral duty of the Han Chinese in general, and for him as an anthropologist in particular, to help them get to the higher level of evolution that they had already reached. To him, that would even the playing field, reduce poverty, poor health and other problems among the ethnic minorities. This is a view of ethnic minorities in China, but it has also been documented a diversity of ethnic identification even among Han Chinese, especially Han settlers in ethnic minority areas (Hansen, 2006).

Research among the ethnic minorities, reveals that they too have a different opinion about their culture and the level of the playing field (Sofield & Li, 2007; Yeh, 2013). However, in several instances liberation meant silencing of cultural traditions. For example, in the 1950s Pingyin, an alphabetised script of Chinese, was developed on the initiative of the government and Naxi children were taught it to learn Mandarin, the newly minted "Esperanto" of China. The Naxi language has later been revitalised

(Poupard, 2019). The Cultural Revolution was a particularly difficult time, as the expression of anything that could even remotely be considered a cultural tradition was violently oppressed, even the Han Chinese traditions. The oppression of the Uighur ethnic minority is the most recent example of the silencing of a cultural tradition through slave labour camps, reducation and forced work migration (Anand, 2019).[2] Another issue, as internationally contentious, is the sinification of Tibet, through the influx of Han Chinese settlers, lack of Tibetan education and strict regulation of local religious practices (Anand, 2019; Yeh, 2013).

In general, it was only when the cultural and historical identification was too different, making it too difficult to meaningfully inscribe a group into the history of imperial or communist China, that the ethnic group was granted a special status. It did not happen of its own accord and the policies of modern China have oscillated between direct oppression, repressive tolerance, and *laissez faire*. There are separate ministries and bureaux that manage relations with ethnic minorities, as well as separate legislation and policies. In the Xi era, the administration has been reorganised and centralised. Anand 2019Yeh 2013 In the institutional hierarchy of the Chinese state, several regions with a high number of minority ethnic groups have the status of Autonomous Regions rather than Provinces. The Party apparatus is frequently less developed in these areas, as is the civil service, and they have different tasks and fewer resources than units in the central areas (Koss, 2018).

The situation of the ethnic minorities in China is too diverse and changing to go into further details (For an updated discussion see Wu, 2019). There is continuous cultural change among the ethnic groups, some drawing closer, others protecting their uniqueness. Processes of continuity and reinvention of tradition still take place today. The key cultural distinction is, and was, between Han and non-Han Chinese.

## The Naxi ethnic minority

The Naxi ethnic minority of about 300,000 people is definitively non-Han Chinese. The main concentration of Naxi is in areas close to the town of Lijiang, in the autonomous Naxi county in Yunnan province. The area lies at the foot of the majestic Jade Dragon Snow Mountain. The brief overview that follows below was first accessed from the homepage of the Naxi Embroidery Institute as this is the clue to the Institute's public self-presentation of the Naxi ethnic identity.[3] I used Google searches to follow up specific details of the various topics and later found an accessible introduction to the group's history and culture, which provides more in-depth background information (Arcones, 2013).

The Naxi speak a Tibetan-Burmese language and have a distinct written language, Dongba. This is a hieroglyphic script with more than 1,500 possible pictograms. It is used together with Geba, a syllabic script used to transcribe mantras and annotate Dongba pictograms to express laws regulating ritual behaviour. Dongba also refers to the Naxi's shamanistic religion influence by Tibetan Buddhism. It is a polytheistic religion with a multitude of gods and spirits. Dongba also refers to priests/shamans, who played a crucial role in conducting rituals, leading chants, and songs memorising traditional knowledge. The shamanistic tradition is carried on through the male line. In a brief video on Youtube, He Xiu Dong claims to have learnt to be a Dongba shaman from his uncle rather than his father, as was the custom. The uncle was a shepherd, who lived very remotely. He had continued his shamanistic practice through the years of repression and was, therefore, able to pass the knowledge on.[4] On the women's side, the tradition continues to manifest in embroidery and textiles, designed according to Dongba cultural rules and tastes.

The community regularly congregate for rituals and festivals, family and village rites of passage, as well as large community-wide celebrations. The Sanduo Festival is still the major celebration, taking place in February/March in a temple area in the Jade Dragon Snow Mountains. Another ritual is the harvest festival in August known as the Torch festival when torches are lit for three days. The festivals are not entirely made up of religious ceremonies as there are also cock, bull and sheep fights, horse-riding competitions, the marketing of goods and produce, eating, dancing, and singing. It is a customary event combining high and low traditions, the transcendent and the immanent. In all, the cultural traditions of the Naxi moral community have been stored and transmitted through several channels: In writing, painting, ritual, poetry and music, cooking, and embroidery.

## The centrally located remote region

The Naxi occupy an economically strategic region at the crossroads between the Southern Silk Road, the mountain passes to the Himalayas, and the roads to Sichuan and the Northern Silk Road. It is also rich in natural resources. The main town is Lijiang, a prefecture-level town with more than one million inhabitants. The Naxi date their history back to at least the 7th century and Lijiang was a centre for international trade for hundreds of years. Its ancient water-supply system secured fresh water and the mix of ecological niches, from the high mountains to the fertile river plains, ensured a steady supply of varied, fresh produce. The strawberries and watermelons that grow in abundance on the plain are still delicacies all over China. Other crops are rice, corn, wheat, potatoes, hemp, and cotton, while husbandry was the major subsistence in the higher altitude areas. The area is also rich in minerals, especially iron and copper.

The area has a highly developed handicraft industry, traditionally excelling in metal, paper, textiles, and leather products. Of particular relevance was the tea trade across the Himalayas, through the "Tea and Horse Route" and the transport of compressed teacakes. The highly sought-after Pu'er tea is produced only in Yunnan and the tea trade was an important part of the Naxi economy. Men would travel with the tea caravans and stay away for months, while the women tended the farms and families. Although in central China it is regarded as a remote and wild area, for hundreds of years, Lijiang and the Naxi region was a melting pot of economic and cultural initiatives in south-west China and Asia.

## A region making use of its competitive advantage

Economically viable for centuries, in the 2000s, the region has again managed to innovate in order to profit from a new trend: The experience economy related to global tourism. Tourism is promoted by the national government as one of the pillars of economic development. For the provincial governments that implement the policies, ethnic minority cultures have thus become an economic resource (Zhang & Lew, 2003), as has the recreational value of nature (Yuan & Wang, 2018). With the market reforms in the Deng era, "ethnic tourism has become a major component of poverty alleviation and social development in western regions of China" (Zhu et al., 2017, p. 733).

The history and location of the Naxi area gives it an international competitive advantage. It has had tourists visiting for decades. At first, the region was the goal of only a trickle of adventurous travellers on private missions. It was part of the British airlift corridor from Burma during the Second World War (1939–1945) and was also used by the US Air Force, and before the PRC, the Communist forces had bases in the area, and so people travelled to revisit. The opium industry was a source of income for many groups over the years. The area was also a departure point for hippie hikers to the fabled Shangri-La. Travellers had to be committed to the task because it took considerable effort to get a travel permit and find transport and lodgings in a remote area with next to nothing in terms of services.

The old town of Lijiang was declared a UNESCO World Cultural Heritage site in 1997.[5] Part of the site is Baisha old town, the centre of the Naxi community between the 7th and 12th centuries and known for its traditional silk embroidery. The area also has national protection as a cultural relic. In 2011, Lijiang, including the famed Leopard Dragon or Yulong Snow Mountain range, was classified as a top-level tourist attraction by the Ministry of Culture and Tourism.[6] The whole region has been under heavy construction in the last two decades. New tarmac roads run along the rivers and new tracks provide easy access to famous river gorges. There is even a town that has laid claim to the Shangri-La name. A cable car takes tourists more than 5,000 m up onto the snow-topped Jade Dragon Mountain. Tea connoisseurs come for the tea experience (Su & Zhang, 2020), and researchers, students, and eco-tourists for the wonders of nature

(Zhang & Lew, 2003), while indigenous tourists come for the ethnic experience (Sofield & Li, 2007).

Tourists are treated with a spectacular Naxi show at a huge amphitheatre, with the Leopard Snow Mountains as a backdrop. Several hundred actors in traditional costumes perform, riding horses, dancing, and singing for mainly Chinese tourists. The show provides a livelihood for many Naxi youths and gives them a chance to exercise their riding, singing, and dancing skills. It is also a place for young Naxi to court, many being tied up in isolated villages for long periods with few opportunities to meet peers. The region is engaged in a thorough and professional innovation initiative: The systematic establishment of an experience economy, in which there is a niche for the Naxi.

## The Baisha Naxi Embroidery Institute

In the midst of this teeming entrepreneurial maelstrom of activity lies the tiny Baisha Naxi Embroidery Institute (hereafter the Institute). It opened for business in 2003 and, although humble in its physical appearance, is thoroughly entangled in international business and art community relations. It is also engaged in social work in the most remote villages of the Naxi community.

I first heard about the Institute from the young writer who commented on the complexity of Chinese society. In the report he gave me, the embroidery Institute is presented as a successful example of a Chinese social enterprise (Zhou et al., 2013). As it was not relevant as a teaching case, I did not think more about it, until more than a year later. While I was on an excursion during a business trip to Yunnan, by sheer luck, the Institute was a stop on a guided bus tour. By then I had been introduced to DEW and the Academy and it struck me how different, yet similar, the Institute was from the two other social enterprises.

A community-run enterprise, the Institute is in a rural village a short drive from Lijiang. The main reason given for its establishment in all available sources was the need to rescue the Naxi artisanal tradition of silk embroidery. Baisha women were adept at a particular silk embroidery technique but, due to decades of cultural repression and modernisation, it was going out of fashion and the knowledge was in danger of being lost. Young adults were more concerned with education and work than investing time and energy in learning to embroider. While traditional embroidery was an important part of the ethnic costume and textiles used for ritual purposes, the embroidery skills themselves had low status, so were not being passed on. Few saw a reason to learn it or wanted to risk the political consequences of being non-Han Chinese. This changed with the Opening Up reforms and especially with the development of tourism and the experience economy.

While there are several other ethnic embroidery workshops and shops in the area and in other ethnic minority areas, the story about the "discovery" of an old tradition is part of a more general indigenous or ethno-tourism trend (Hinch & Butler, 2007). Social enterprises based on reinvention and commodification of local artisanal tradition are also a common pattern in other countries (Borges Ladeira & Vier Machado, 2013), as are social enterprises drawing on spiritual traditions (Fonneland, 2012) and ethnic entrepreneurship in general (Krogstad, 2004). Whatever the initial drive, many of these social entrepreneurs take social responsibility, stand up for injustice and work to improve conditions for the disadvantaged. In this sense, the Institute is going by the book. Like other social enterprises in the global movement, it grew out of a particular arts and crafts tradition and carved out an existence for itself in the complex institutional landscape of China.

### *The government model enterprise*

The Institute is of particular interest in case of China because of its role in continuing the moral economy of the Naxi. Even so, it is a model enterprise according to the government's Leninist governance system. On its home page the awards are proudly displayed. As such, it is a showpiece for the government and firmly situated within the Han Chinese system of governance. The Institute is well connected to national elite art institutions and great care has gone into shaping the design, colouring and pattern of the embroidery to adapt it to current tastes. Naxi intellectuals, through their research publications and responses to state policies, preserve and revitalise Naxi culture (Yu, 2009). The Institute is also a receptor for Naxi cultural traditions, a place where ethnic traditions gain legitimacy nationally and internationally.

During my visit, one of the embroidery teachers gave us a guided tour. She explained that the Naxi embroidery style is of a naturalistic, 3D-like quality. Silk threads are split to less than a hair's breadth and then part woven, part sown according to detailed drawings. The use of silk thread produces a unique gleam in the embroidery. The guide-cum-seller in the shop, demonstrated the difference between typical tourist and true art pieces. There are also observable differences between the Han Chinese-inspired and the Dongba designs. The Han Chinese-inspired pieces were of typical scenes in Chinese arts: Lotus and peonies, cloud-topped mountains, and pagodas along waterfalls. There was even one with an exquisite painting of Mao Zedong. President Xi Jinping also had his portrait embroidered, I was told. The Dongba belonged with the naïve art style, simple in patterns and motif, displaying vases, vessels or people, and shaped in pictogram style. The colouring was different, with less lustrous, earthier, cloudy hues. The efforts of the lead artists in developing unique, yet typical, designs were apparent.

Those responsible for developing new designs are renowned artists themselves, prominently introduced at the Institute's homepage. The

Institute's main art consultant is accomplished contemporary painter Zhang Chun He. Regarded as the creator of modern Dongba painting. He is a Naxi himself.[7] A graduate of the Beijing Central Academy of National Minorities, he is vice-chairman of the Association for the Promotion of Dongba Art and Culture and vice-chairman of the International Society of Naxi studies. He is also represented at international exhibitions in Germany, Mexico, Israel, Singapore, and in large cities in China. Another accomplished artist is the institute's Principal Xu Yunkui, a renowned woodblock painter and member of the National Art and Literature Association.[8] The master embroiderer Mo Meiyuan is the embroidery headmistress.[9] She has passed on the artisanal skills to young Naxi embroidery students, who not only learn the embroidery skills but also the Dongba aesthetics and symbolic meaning of the forms and colours in the embroideries.[10] The Institute also has connections with a shaman, He Zhengwen.[11] As a 24th generation Naxi Dongba shaman he is the in-house expert on the intangible Naxi heritage. He is also listed as a member of the Yunnan Artists Association.

As types of stakeholders, the artists and artisans of the Institute fill the positions of society but also of managers, so that they cross the boundary between internal and external stakeholders. They also mediate between government and society when engaged in the various GONGO-positions. By filling these positions, they are reinventing the Naxi artistic tradition and representing it beyond the local level. They also reposition the Naxi ethnic minority culture.

### *The commercial enterprise in the experience economy*

Tourists mean a steady income and connection between the Institute and the international market. The Naxi cultural basis is as important a selling point to tourists as the quality of its embroidery. It has an accessible web page in both Chinese and English and international travel websites and blogs give it frequent and positive reviews. The products are high-quality and the service quick and reliable, resulting in products that are expensive but worth the money. Internationally, the institute has a visible digital market presence.

The Institute also makes use of its position in the ethno-tourism development of the area. Even though the village where the Institute is located is a stop on the regular tour circuit of the many tour operators in the area, it was far less crowded than other sites. That was how it was presented at the tour I had the luck of attending. The little nondescript village at first seemed to be just another of the many attractions on the tour, an opportunity to get close to the real China. As we walked down the lanes of an apparently vibrant local village, the guide stopped at a nice red entrance, where a passage led into an open-air yard enclosed by pavilion-like houses. The building enhanced the feeling of entering a traditional Chinese dwelling, but the stories told were about the Naxi embroidery traditions, silk and its role in the Naxi textile tradition, and the technical details of the embroidery. The story of the near loss of the embroidery tradition and how the skills were now being taught to the young was told in the workshop, where busy embroiderers demonstrated their technical skills.

The public space of the Institute consisted of the workshop, where we could observe the embroidery process and exchange some words with the weavers; the gallery, where items for sale were displayed; a small area for woodblock carving; and a little museum. The tour ended in the shop, where large, refined embroideries were displayed along with small affordable pieces. The invitation to buy a souvenir was unmistakable, although discreet and friendly. I learnt more about the Naxi aesthetic tradition from people situated strategically in the different rooms.

After the visit to the Institute, we had an hour or so to stroll through the village. This strengthened my impression of a village with a life of its own, not merely an attraction that would close down when the tourists left for the day. Women in colourful dresses walked down the street, while children ran around playing and men sat on stools along the walls of the traditional houses. With dogs slinking around the corners, clucking hens and weeds waving in the wind, it was like any rural village. The savoury lunch of traditional Naxi dishes completed the experience. Although there were far fewer tourists here than in Lijiang, I recognised the strange invisible social wall that protects locals in places invaded by tourists from my youth in a similar setting. Tourism here was simply an add-on to village life. The Naxi culture was very much a living tradition. They looked at us and we looked at them, but our task was to be tourists: Visit the monuments, take pictures, and buy souvenirs. Spend money and then leave. The moral economy of the Naxi, however, still constituted its backbone, not the productivist economic principles.

Ethno-tourism is by no means unproblematic. It is contested for many reasons, leading one author to comment that it produces "edited" versions of minority culture (Hillman, 2003, p. 185). The Institute, clearly embedded in the institutionally complex net of relations with the ethnic majority and the international market, is nevertheless a manifestation of the moral economy. Earning money from artefacts and managing events for tourists is also an opportunity to reinvent or even continue traditions. In a study of traditional drawings, the researcher concluded that:

> In addition to being visualisations of how rural ethnic China is imagined by and for urban tourists, these renderings are indicative of the competing ambitions at stake for village residents and contribute to the reformulation, and potential resignification, of the very tropes evoked by the drawings themselves. (Chio, 2017, p. 419)

### *The social impact*

The Institute is not using social tourism to attract resources. Social tourism refers to travel organised for people with disabilities and for visits to people with disabilities. The term is contested, as is the practice (Mao & Liu, 2014; Minnaert et al., 2011). However, the Institute is deeply involved in social work, in addition to its engagement in commerce, arts and policymaking.

The Institute also works to meet the social needs of individuals in remote, rural villages. During my visit, I was surprised to see a young man embroidering at one of the embroidery tables, otherwise, all occupied by women. Naxi embroidery had been presented as women's work, so how was it that a young male had chosen and been accepted to learn such a gendered skill? Our guide, herself a master embroiderer, explained that the Institute had started to teach embroidery to handicapped young people from the villages, including young men, who could find no other means of providing for themselves or establishing their own families. He was not the only one. The story of another is displayed on the homepage. The student was lame from poliomyelitis. His handicap left him with few opportunities for work in his village. His lack of access to education likewise left him with no opportunities for employment in town. He started to learn embroidery at the Institute in 2015 and is now capable of making a living as well as teaching others.

It takes years to become a master embroiderer. The Institute has grants for Naxi village students too poor to pay for the education. Room and board are included in the tuition. The students stay from months to years to learn to embroider. After getting a vocational education at the Institute, those who qualify are certified to go back to their villages to teach embroidery to others. The Institute has so far set up seven Naxi community classrooms and two classrooms in the so-called immigrant villages. Graduates who show promise are allowed to embroider gradually more complex pieces. The embroidery is then sold at the Institute's gallery shop. Small cloths embroidered with a simple flower or house by a river are mass produced for tourists. Larger and more complex embroideries are sought after but expensive. Sale of the textiles provides the Institute with a steady income. This makes the Institute into a for-profit enterprise. The customers are tourists, and the Institute the supplier of merchandise. It is a classic market economy set-up. However, internally the students are not employees, and the managers not managers in the business sense. In the artisanal tradition, they are masters teaching the bachelors their craft. They do not work for wages; they are engaged in handicraft production and earn their keep. The Naxi ethnic customs mediate this business model. Profit is not the goal. Its social mission is to revive the Naxi embroidery tradition, and to provide handicapped Naxi youth with the means to make a living. The social mission goes hand in hand with the deeper cultural mission. The Institute operates in a distinct moral economy, which it perpetuates by its activities.

## Summing up

The Institute operates across several economic spheres but is foremost embedded in the moral economy of the Naxi community. The Naxi moral economy is a separate part of China's political economy. Because of the loose border between them and the far larger domestic economy, the transformative powers of social enterprises operating here is potent, yet they remain separate. The enterprise makes a difference, directly for the beneficiaries, handicapped youth and women, and indirectly by raising awareness and respect for the Naxi, a marginalised group in China, giving it centre stage, and prospering in the process.

## Notes

1 China statistical yearbook, 2019. http://www.stats.gov.cn/tjsj/ndsj/2019/indexeh.htm
2 Xu, V. X., Cave, D., Leibold, J., Munro, K., & Ruser, N. (2020). Uyghurs for sale | Australian Strategic Policy Institute | ASPI. https://www.aspi.org.au/report/uyghurs-sale. In *Australian Strategic Policy Institute*.
3 http://www.lijiangethnicembroidery.com/en/h-about.html
4 He, Ziu Dong. 2018. Forgotten Kingdom: Dongba Shaman – He Xiu Dong [Yunnan, China]. https://www.youtube.com/watch?v=uFqphmFTJy8. Accessed January 11, 2021.
5 UNESCO. 1997. Old Town of Lijiang. https://whc.unesco.org/en/list/811/. Accessed March 13, 2021.
6 China Daily, July 7, 2011. Lijiang ancient town licenced national 5A tourism attraction spot. https://www.chinadaily.com.cn/travel/2011-07/28/content_13002046.htm. Accessed March 13, 2021.
7 Nau, Michel (undated). Zhang, Chunhe. https://www.chinesenewart.com/chinese-artists5/zhangchunhe.htm. Accessed March 13, 2021.
8 https://www.yunnanexploration.com/xu-yunkui-printmaking-artist-in-lijiang.html Accessed March 13, 2021.
9 https://www.yunnanexploration.com/momeiyan-grand-master-and-the-embroidery-preceptor-of-the-institute.html. Accessed March 13, 2021.
10 http://m.lijiangethnicembroidery.com/en/nd.jsp?id=245. Accessed March 13, 2021.
11 https://www.yunnanexploration.com/he-zhengwensenior-dongba-intangible-culture-inheritor.html. Accessed March 13, 2021.

## References

Adelman, J. (2020). Introduction: The moral economy, the careers of a concept. *Humanity Journal*, *11*(2), 187–192.

Anand, D. (2019). Colonization with Chinese characteristics: Politics of (in)security in Xinjiang and Tibet. *Central Asian Survey*, 38(1), 129–147. https://doi.org/10.1080/02634937.2018.1534801

Arcones, R. P. C. (2013). Sons of heaven, brothers of nature. *The Naxi of Southwest China*. CreateSpace Independent Publishing Platform.

Borges Ladeira, F. M., & Vier Machado, H. (2013). Social entrepreneurship: A reflection for adopting public policies that support the third sector in Brazil.

*Journal of Technology Management & Innovation*, *8*(1), 1–17. https://doi.org/10.4067/S0718-27242013000300017

Brøgger, B. unpublished. *Business as usual: Business, morality and adaption among the Chinese in Penang*. Malaysia. Mag.art. thesis, Department of Social Anthreopology, University of Oslo.

Chio, J. (2017). Rendering rural modernity: Spectacle and power in a Chinese ethnic tourism village. *Critique of Anthropology*, *37*(4), 418–439. https://doi.org/10.1177/0308275X17735368

Dikötter, F. (Ed.). (1997). *Racial discourse in China: Continuities and permutations*. Hong Kong University Press.

Fonneland, T. (2012). Spiritual Entrepreneurship in a Northern Landscape: Spirituality, Tourism and Politics. *Temenos – Nordic Journal of Comparative Religion*, *48*(2), 155–178. https://doi.org/10.33356/temenos.7510

Götz, N. (2015). 'Moral economy': Its conceptual history and analytical prospects. *Journal of Global Ethics*, *11*(2), 147–162. https://doi.org/10.1080/17449626.2015.1054556

Hallgren, C. (1986). *Morally united and politically divided: The Chinese community of Penang*. Department of Social Anthropology, University of Stockholm.

Hansen, M. H. (2006). *Frontier people: Han settlers in minority areas of China*. University of British Columbia Press.

Hillman, B. (2003). Paradise under construction: Minorities, myths and modernity in Northwest Yunnan. *Asian Ethnicity*, *4*(2), 177–190. https://doi.org/10.1080/14631360301654

Hinch, T., & Butler, R. (2007). Introduction: Revisiting common ground. In R. Butler & T. Hinch (Eds.), *Tourism and indigenous peoples: Issues and implications* (pp. 1–14). Butterworth-Heinemann.

Koss, D. (2018). *Where the party rules: The rank and file of China's communist state*. Cambridge University Press.

Krogstad, A. (2004). From Chop Suey to Sushi, Champagne, and VIP Lounge: Culinary entrepreneurship through two generations. *Social Analysis*, *48*(1), 196–217. https://doi.org/10.3167/015597704782352708

Manger, L. (2013). Chapter 11 Building a moral economy: The historical success of Hadrami Sada in Singapore. In E. Bråten (Ed.), *Embedded entrepreneurship: Market, culture, and micro-business in Insular Southeast Asia* (pp. 235–251). BRILL. 10.1163/9789004255296_012

Mao, H. Y., & Liu, X. (2014). Research on the development of China's social tourism. *Advanced Materials Research*, *926–930*, 3910–3913. https://doi.org/10.4028/www.scientific.net/AMR.926-930.3910

Minnaert, L., Maitland, R., & Miller, G. (2011). What is social tourism? *Current Issues in Tourism*, *14*(5), 403–415. https://doi.org/10.1080/13683500.2011.568051

O'Brien, K. J., & Li, L. (2006). *Rightful resistance in rural China*. Cambridge University Press. https://doi.org/10.1017/CBO9780511791086

Poupard, D. (2019). Revitalising Naxi dongba as a 'pictographic' vernacular script. *Journal of Chinese Writing Systems*, *3*(1), 53–67. https://doi.org/10.1177/2513850218814405

Scott, J. C. (1976). *The moral economy of the peasant: Rebellion and subsistence in Southeast Asia*. Yale Univ. Press.

Sofield, T., & Li, F. M. S. (2007). Chapter 19 Indigenous minorities of China and effects of tourism. In T. Hinch & R. Butler (Eds.), *Tourism and indigenous peoples* (pp. 265–280). Butterworth-Heinemann.

Su, X., & Zhang, H. (2020). *Tea drinking and the tastescapes of wellbeing in tourism. Tourism Geographies*, 1–21. https://doi.org/10.1080/14616688.2020.1750685

Thompson, E. P. (1971). The moral economy of the English crowd in the 18th century. *Past and Present*, *50*(1), 76–136. https://doi.org/10.1093/past/50.1.76

Wilson, D., & Dixon, W. (2014). *A history of "Homo Economicus": The nature of the moral in economic theory*. Routledge.

Wu, G. (2019). *Narrating Southern Chinese minority nationalities*. Springer, Singapore. https://doi.org/10.1007/978-981-13-6022-0_1

Yeh, E. T. (2013). *Taming Tibet: Landscape transformation and the gift of Chinese development*. Cornell University Press.

Yu, H. (2009). *Identity and schooling among the Naxi: Becoming Chinese with Naxi identity*. Lexington Books.

Yuan, L.-l., & Wang, S.-j. (2018). Recreational value of glacier tourism resources: A travel cost analysis for Yulong Snow Mountain. *Journal of Mountain Science*, *15*(7), 1446–1459. https://doi.org/10.1007/s11629-017-4685-4

Zhang, G., & Lew, A. A. (2003). Chapter 1 China's Tourism Boom. In A. A. Lew, L. Yu, J. Ap, & G. Zhang (Eds.), *Tourism in China* (pp. 3–11). Haworth Hospitality Press.

Zhou, W., Zhu, X., Qiu, T., Yuan, R., Chen, J., Chen., T. (2013). *China Social Enterprise and Impact Investment Report*. English language version edited by David Hayward Evans, and translated by Manning Ding. Shanghai University of Finance & Economics Social Enterprise Research Center,Peking University Center for Civil Society Studies, the 21st Century SocialInnovation Research Center, and the University of Pennsylvania School ofSocial Policy & Practice. https://www.ubs.com/global/en/ubs-society/philanthropy/resources//china-social-enterprise-and-investment-report-aug-2013-en.pdf

Zhu, Y., Jin, L., & Graburn, N. (2017). Domesticating tourism anthropology in China. *American Anthropologist*, *119*(4), 730–735. https://doi.org/10.1111/aman.12956

# 6 A socialist economy with Chinese characteristics

The trajectory that China's leaders follow is towards socialism. The twist and turns in the road are a pressing ideological concern, discussed in terms of what a socialist economy with Chinese characteristics is. The discussion has been complicated with the turn to a market economy (Gong & Cortese, 2017). Even if there is no agreement as to the details, the main direction is undisputed among China's leaders, and hence this vision frames every social initiative, including that of social enterprises. They are assessed according to their role in realising this vision or, at least, they must be able to somehow demonstrate that their operations contribute to it. As a domesticated foreign import, the social enterprise that survives has managed this in different ways, as illustrated in the three previous chapters. A number of other enterprises are caught in the middle of conflicting views on the trajectory as well. I will focus on three types: State-owned enterprises (SOEs), rural cooperative economic organisations, and religious communities. Each of these was at some point part of China's welfare system and still have considerable social impact.

Before the PRC, religious communities were important, if informal, parts of the social security system. Even though they were banned during the Mao era, they continued to exist and provide health and social services. When the PRC came into being, SOEs took over some of the burden. The main body of SOEs was established in the 1950s as part of the PRC's industrialisation policies. SOEs provided their workers with cradle-to-grave mandatory social services. Although the political regime has changed, the SOEs are still important providers of social services. With the market reform in the Deng era, a large number of SOEs were dismantled. This has had both productive and unproductive consequences. Productive because many unemployed local managers and party cadres started enterprises, which have been a driving force for rural entrepreneurship. Unproductive because many people lost their social safety net, which has increased social needs. Although not typical social enterprises, SOEs, rural economic organisations and religious communities are part of the social enterprise landscape. They provide alternatives vistas of the social contract and how it changes. The SOE is a model type of enterprise within the government's

DOI: 10.4324/9780429282591-6

vision of a socialist economy with Chinese characteristics. The rural economic organisations are crucial for the realisation of productivist social innovation policies. The religious communities do not enjoy political favour but are important in everyday life. In their different ways, all three types of enterprises meet social needs. An account of the transformative powers of social enterprise in China is therefore incomplete without them.

## State-owned enterprises (SOEs)

In the 1950s, after more than 30 years of war, industry in China was geared towards supplying various war efforts. With the PRC, it had to adapt to peacetime consumption patterns. All industry was nationalised and SOEs were established in the 1950s as part of urgently needed reconstruction and development. Although personnel and equipment were available, the challenge was to distribute them. Building materials were commissioned from central shops as well as local sources, by force if necessary. Central plans determined the number and types of industries, and low-tech industries in energy, ore, metalwork, and machinery were deemed crucial. Although natural resources such as electricity, mineral deposits, and transport were considered, there was a preference for areas where the Party was well established and where the communists had a good underground network or had been liberated early by the PLA. The PLA continued its central role in the SOEs until well into the Deng era (Mulvenon, 2000). Able personnel, chosen from the People's Liberation Army (PLA) and the civilian cadre within the Communist Party, were sent to survey conditions for new industries.

The movement of people in various reform periods of the SOEs has similarities with the industrialisation process in the UK in the 1500s to 1700s, which produced what was later known as the proletariat. A large floating population came into existence after the privatisation of former communal grazing land, in which the "enclosure" policy had forced millions of smallholders off the land (Polanyi, 2001). In China the process was much quicker and peasants turned into workers overnight. Control of the means of production remained with the CCP and it was executed through a strictly planned, politically controlled economy. In line with the rural economy of China, Mao Zedong revised communist ideology to include the peasants as the "proletariat." Workers were hired, factories built and machinery and equipment commissioned. Due to demilitarisation, radical land reforms, and political campaigns against the capitalist class, there was no shortage of workers.

Political connections and academic merit, especially in fields like engineering and the natural sciences, were the main criteria for getting a position as a manager of an SOE. The internal management structure in the enterprises included a parallel hierarchy of political agents and management (Wang, 2014). Local networks and connections in the Party was the basis for recruitment and advancement. There was neither a body of professionally trained managers nor business schools for training them. Training took place at the Party schools.

Unlike the factories of early Western industrialisation, SOEs were set up according to the Maoist principle of "cradle to grave" commitment. It provided the population with an "iron rice bowl." It did indeed provide rice but its grip was as hard as iron. Hence, these enterprises did not only answer to their owners regarding their productivity and profitability but also the wellbeing of their workers and staff: "A typical SOE … was established as a mini-community with all social service facilities, such as a canteen, a medical clinic, a beauty salon, a theatre, and shuttle buses" (Bai et al., 2000, p. 718). Hence, SOEs were charged with seeing to the social needs of workers as well as production proper. For many years most SOEs were like fully functioning towns. At least, that was how they operated until their dismantling in the Deng era.

### *Social problems and managerial competence*

Western academics and policy advisors recommended the dismantling of SOEs. According to their macro and micro-economic calculations, SOEs were inefficient, lost money and were a heavy burden on national finances (Lin et al., 2020). The Chinese government carefully and gradually changed policies regulating the operations of SOEs, using the same gradual approach as with the Special Economic Zone in Shenzhen. The dismantling began about the same time. The unintended consequences were a rapid increase in social problems and opportunities for commercial entrepreneurs. Social entrepreneurs came late in this process, outlined as follows. Lin and her colleagues identified five stages of change from 1978 to today, and I use the same timeline below. The stages span the Deng and Xi decades, and the intermediate years between the Mao and the Deng era, when the Maoist influences were still strong.

Stage 1 (1978–1984). The first step in the market reform of the SOEs was to loosen ties between SOEs and centrally determined production plans. SOEs gained extended rights to make operational decisions and keep part of their profits. This reform did not considerably affect the situation for workers or the local communities where SOEs were located, while the government gained experience as professional owners in the market economy meaning of the term.

Stage 2 (1984–1992). In these years, the relationship between the government and SOEs changed into a more business-like contractual relationship. This policy was called the contract responsibility system. Managers gained rights to profits in excess of a predetermined level for three to five years. This increased incentives for quick wins, short-term projects that paid off quickly, rather than the heavy, long-term investments required to upgrade many worn-down factories. One way to ensure a quick win was to lay off workers. This policy change had considerable effect on the local population. There was neither bowl nor rice available for the unemployed or their families, iron or not. This was especially problematic as the government decided to discontinue many of the social security funds and institutions established during the Mao era (Pan, 2017) and reinstate a market governance mechanism.

The contract responsibility system has similarities with the "revenue farm system" known from South-East Asia in the 1800s. In this system,

> The government granted a private contractor, the revenue farmer, the exclusive right to collect a certain tax in a specified area for a set number of years in return for a fixed rent, and the farmer kept for himself any money which he collected over and above what he owed the government in rent. (Butcher, 1983, p. 387)

In South-East Asia, ethnic Chinese stakeholder groups, kongsis or secret societies as the colonial governments called them, bid on the right to collect taxes from the Chinese population, a huge body of mostly male migrant workers, known as coolies. The winning association kept part of the surplus. The associations used the surplus on social services, insurance schemes, schools, and hospitals, which were not provided by the colonial government. Unlike the tax farming mechanism, the contract responsibility system was revised after only a few years.

Stage 3 (1992–2002): This period saw the most systematic establishment of a modern enterprise system. Internal management structures were thoroughly redesigned and supporting external institutions, financial regulations, and institutions were established. However, they depended on an immature financial system (Park & Sehrt, 2001). During this time, roughly 65 million SOE workers lost their jobs (Elfstrom, 2020), and social unrest built-up (Bai et al., 2000). It also opened up new business opportunities, which led to other problems: "Quality assets were captured by the non-state sector due to weak law enforcement. Such entrenchment activities became an increasingly prominent problem, causing social dissatisfaction" (Lin et al., 2020, p. 28). On the positive side, the layoffs resulted in the build-up of managerial competence and assets in the local and private sector (Lin et al., 2020), and the strengthening of rural entrepreneurship (Dai et al., 2019).

Stage 4 (2003–2012): Three crucial national policy changes occurred. The first was the separation of SOEs into more or less nationally and strategically important ones. The large ones came under central-level institutions, while lower-level agencies governed the smaller, less critical ones. The second change was the implementation of a new internal governance structure for SOEs. The boards of directors were separated from the top management team and recruitment to the governing bodies was based more on a manager's functions than connections. To some extent this weakened the influence of the established national patron–client systems and left local governing bodies to deal with social unrest. The third change was the implementation of counteracting policies that re-established government-funded social benefit schemes of various kinds, revised social policy reforms and initiated a vast number of poverty alleviation projects.

In the Xi era, from 2012, there have again been extensive SOE reforms, reversing a number of earlier changes by *de facto* giving the Party committees firmer control and cadre positions in the SOEs' governing bodies, on the one hand, and expansion into the international markets on the other:

> The state-owned Assets Supervision and Administration Commission (SASAC) was established as a specialised third party for supervising and guiding the major decisions and activities of SOEs. Although the state appeared to visibly withdraw from the running of operations, central control over SOEs was tactically preserved via SASAC's political instructions embedded in performance evaluation benchmarks, personnel appointments and employment rules, and the enterprise's investment proposal. (Li & Soobaroyen, 2021, p. 12)

In 2017, 75 of the 102 SOEs on the Fortune 500 list were Chinese owned. The number of true SOEs, defined as "non-corporation economic units, where the entire assets are owned by the state," was about 130,000.[1] The number is even higher when limited liability corporations are included.

Today top management of the top SOEs have ministerial ranking and considerable influence on the operations of the enterprises. They "hold the commanding heights of state control advocated by Vladimir Lenin" (Lin et al., 2020, p. 33). The researchers point out that these managers bear a heavy political burden and soft budget constraints. While fiscal subsidies and tax cuts for the enterprise in case of problems is more likely than for a private limited liability corporation, managers have to find ways to meet social needs and support local social stability.

## *SOEs as functional towns*

An SOE is like the keep of a mediaeval castle, surrounded by walls, with guarded entry points. During a visit to a small SOE in a remote area, I found this an apt metaphor. Inside the estate were, of course, all the functional units necessary to operate the factories but, in addition, there were all the institutions required to keep a society running: Stores, nurseries, schools, hospitals, entertainment, and elderly care. An engineer who had been with the surveying team for the establishment of the SEO in the 1950s explained how the team had identified abundant raw material and energy sources, which compensated for the remote location. Transport would be expensive but still worth the investment he explained. From a window high up in one of the apartment blocks of the SOE's housing compound, he made a sweeping gesture over the landscape, indicating the rivers, mountains, and soil that had made the construction of the SOE possible.

Educated abroad in the 1950s, the engineer had held an important managerial position in the SOE until a fallout with the government during the Cultural Revolution. He and his family lost all privileges, but he later regained them. His son was employed in the administration in the 1990s and was now nearing pension age. Both were safe in their social rights, with access to their own apartments and available social benefits. Yet both had observed the dismantling of the social services and were not happy with what they saw. The nursery and schools on the compound had closed down and the hospital was about to. With the limited resources available, the regional government had chosen to invest in new transport infrastructure and the upgrading of production facilities. Clearly in support of the engineering side of the enterprise, the grandfather was particularly worried about the deteriorating social conditions.

Although worn down, the compound that housed some 5,000 inhabitants, was neat and well-tended. The security was efficient, the greenery along the walkways lush and the elevators worked. During the day, chatting elderly people occupied every bench and stool. What was eerie, was the quiet in the evenings. There was no hustle and bustle of workers returning home from work. The compound appeared to be a community that would disappear with its elderly residents.

The community life in the streets surrounding the compound, however, was a stark contrast. Rows and rows of hawkers' stalls and small shops ran along the compound walls and around a large, government-regulated fresh market. Commercial activity began before sunrise and lasted until well after supper. The market was served by farmers coming in from the surrounding countryside with their produce, retail traders peddling their goods, and small family operated businesses. The SOE was at the centre of this teeming economic activity. This experience resonates with what other researchers have found: "The conclusion that a certain proportion of SOEs should continue to exist during reform is driven by the condition that the government cannot find other means to provide a social safety net for unemployed workers" (Bai et al., 2000, p. 718) and to add, provide a nexus for small-scale market transactions that provide people with the means for making a living. So far, neither the public health or social welfare apparatus nor social enterprises are enough to meet the needs.

### *Corporate social responsibility*

Contrary to giant corporations in other countries, corporate social responsibility was part of the SOEs raison d'etre from the beginning. In China, the SOE reform actually served to wean them from their social responsibilities. Still, they are important for employment, environmental protection, and corporate philanthropic giving, and the SOEs are legally required to implement CSR policies (Cao, 2017).

All but the most strategically positioned SOEs grapple with the for-profit or social mission dilemma. Unlike other companies, however, they have to deal with a well-organised, very legitimate force of resistance, the workers. Even after large lay-offs still about 60 million people are employed in SOEs. A rough estimate based on an average household size of three people means that SOEs provide livelihoods and economic safety for more than a quarter of a million people. Unrest among the workers and their organisations directly affects not only economic productivity but also social stability (Elfstrom, 2020).

In spite of years of training in professional business management methods, managers use access to social benefits as a management tool more in line with Leninist teachings. Unproductive or unpopular workers may be deprived of social benefits like holidays, health care, or housing maintenance. Such practices increase public scepticism towards the reforms. In tense situations, the SOEs past role as frontrunners for the economic revolution is a double-edged sword. SOEs have Cultural Revolution heroes, military veterans, experienced managers, all with leadership experience and deep knowledge of how the Chinese polity works. They live in the local communities with connections to local political bodies. They are a powerful force of resistance against unwanted government policies. Local government officials take care to meet resisting workers to mediate with and preferably win over by argument and deliberation, rather than brute force. Strikes are less likely to end in arrests at SEOs than at private companies. Social responsibility is still strong, and this has consequences for the operations of SEOs.

A managerial problem is that in many cases the products from SOEs are not in demand and of poor quality. This is commonly attributed to the fact that resources are used for what in economics is defined as unproductive activities: "In a typical Chinese SOE, the ratio of welfare-provision assets, such as company housing, company-run childcare and schools, and sports facilities, to total assets reaches 35 to 40%. Welfare benefits in monetary form account for over 50% of the total wage bill" (Bai et al., 2000, p. 721). In terms of shareholder profit, this may be less than ideal. In terms of social impact, however, it may not be such a bad achievement – if the quality of the social services is up to standard.

## Rural cooperative economic organisations

Enterprising rural villagers have lifted millions out of poverty. In starting up their enterprises, they mobilise local resources, such as the skills and connections of other villagers, land, and local capital. When an enterprise succeeds, it creates jobs and engages with other local enterprises so that the economic benefits have a ripple effect. This is the textbook understanding of entrepreneurship generally. When this happens in villages, it is defined as rural entrepreneurship, and this in turn is regarded as a form of social entrepreneurship. This is why a discussion of social enterprises in China is incomplete without assessing the role of rural start-ups.

In the Mao era, farmer and commune enterprises were promoted from around the 1960s, when the Soviet economic model was abandoned and the Maoist principle of peasants as the leading force of the revolution was introduced (Mao, 1965). With the introduction of the people's commune as the main rural social unit, a number of communal enterprises were also set up, such as communal dairies or poultry farms or processing plants for speciality produce. Embroiled in local political strife, with untrained managers and poorly equipped, many did not succeed or were simply abandoned. This changed when the communes were disbanded and replaced with the household contractual responsibility system formally legalised in the early 1980s (Patnaik, 1987). Although land was still communally owned, households were allowed to keep the yield from their share of land, after having paid taxes to the state and fees for collective services to the local government. A number of communal tasks and non-land resources became available for a new kind of entrepreneur.

### *Township and Village Enterprises (TVE)*

A pull towards setting up enterprises were the unused productive resources resulting from the market economy reforms that had also left a number of local party cadres and managers unemployed. They started enterprises of their own. In addition, due to migration pattern and urbanization, village leaders and villagers were crucial personnel. Rural enterprises that had been started in the Mao era, provided the groundwork for a new type of business that appeared in the Deng era, the Township and Village Enterprise (TVE). They grew rapidly and then faded out again after a couple of decades (Park & Shen, 2003). When the TVE company form was recognised in 1984, the number of factories being set up in local villages increased rapidly. Some were based on agricultural needs, like fertiliser and insecticide plants. Others were needed for infrastructure upgrading, brick-and-tile makers, cement production, and mechanical industry, while others produced garments or coal for local use. A number of tasks again required collaboration and were better solved communally than by individual households. Such tasks provided opportunities for rural entrepreneurship and village enterprises.

TVEs were neither state-owned enterprises or cooperatives, nor private enterprises, but "a collection of community enterprises with a governance structure in which the community government has control" (Che & Qian, 1998, p. 2). Community in this context may refer to one or more villages, townships, or a combination of both. Profits were shared between villagers, workers, and the local government according to explicit rules. The communal profits were then used for local public goods such as schools, roads, and irrigation. The enterprises had little access to government funds, but there were some advantages to having the local government as part of the enterprise as it could ease access to public funds (Park & Shen, 2003). Many of the early entrepreneurs had little or no knowledge of operating a factory or a business and many ventures failed (Lin & Xie, 2018). These initiatives provided the villagers with experiences that became useful as the social innovation policies were strengthened (Dai et al., 2019). In many cases, proceeds were reinvested in the local economy to establish factories or improve agriculture, and to upgrade local infrastructure, schools, and health services – all investments that had considerable social impact.

### *The dark side of rural entrepreneurship*

Rural entrepreneurship has not been an all-positive experience. Land reforms led to the sale of communal land. Local village leaders and party cadres sold land, in many cases despite the protests of farmers, who only had usury rights to the fields and lost their livelihood. The intertwining of ownership rights and management structures opened up a huge grey area where local cadres and village leaders were able to sell communal land and pocket the profit or fulfil tax quotas (Whiting, 2000). At times, whole villages would be against the sale of communal land, to little avail. The sale of farmland was pushed by a series of housing and construction booms beginning in the 1990s. As land prices soared, the corruption problem escalated. After the 1990s, corruption and contested land sales became the most common sources of local political protests in China (O'Brien & Li, 2006).

An institution that was and is frequently used to protest is the "letters and visits" tradition. This allows people with a grievance to make a written appeal to the relevant level of government and gives them the chance to be heard at a meeting, the "visit," often couched in terms of "having a cup of tea" to check out the situation. (It has similarities to the situation described in Chapter 4 about the Academy lunch, where a local Party secretary happened to "drop by" for a chat). Many grievances are sorted out through this quasi-formal deliberative mechanism. If claims are not properly addressed this way, protesters take them to the next level of government and, if necessary, all the way to central level. Most cases are dealt with at the local level. O'Brien and Li reported that several hundred claims were nudged through the convoluted government system all the way to the central level.

Another mediating mechanism is a new type of rural entrepreneur, the "peasant lawyer" (Brandtstädter, 2020). Peasant lawyers are concerned citizens who help peasants with their legal claims. They are without formal education but have extensive practical knowledge of the legal system (Brandtstädter, 2020). The result of the various pushes and pulls is that rural entrepreneurship, activism, and social entrepreneurship are nearly indistinguishable in China. Although the reduction of poverty and of rural inequality is a national development goal, the very local nature of rural entrepreneurship meant that it was long an untamed force. However, it was gradually included in the national innovation system as the government allocated resources to social innovation by redirecting the NIS-system towards rural entrepreneurship (Wu et al., 2017), thus connecting locals' efforts to improve their lot with central efforts through macro-economic development policies.

### *Private collectivisation*

As conditions for private enterprises improved in the 1990s, the number of TVEs rapidly declined (Kung & Lin, 2007) and "by the turn of the century, the town and village enterprises were well on their way to becoming conventional firms" (McMillan & Woodruff, 2002, p. 165). At the same time, experiments with various models of economic cooperative associations continued unabated, hence the collective platform of privatisation was also developed (Whiting, 2000). In one community, the village committee took the lead in the innovation process, in another it was volunteers, and in a third the village enterprise (Pan, 2017, pp. 151–161). The strengthening of a predominantly urban privatisation process was matched by a predominantly rural re-collectivisation drive in support of rural community construction after the "hollowing out" of local communities in the first decades of the Opening Up reforms. In a comparative study of four villages that succeeded in turning the tide, the authors find a combination of mobilisation of external government and business networks. Local elite support is as important for lasting results as location and access to natural and human resources (Li et al., 2019). Digitalisation has strengthened this trend and resulted in remigration back to the villages. The most prominent example of an organizational, even societal, innovation based on the new technology is the Taobao villages (Cui et al., 2017; Wei et al., 2020). In 2019, a public estimate was that 10 million people were engaged in e-commerce-based rural entrepreneurship.[2]

When the government clamped down on corruption from 2012, this was seen as a manoeuvre by President Xi to consolidate his hold on power but that may be too simplistic an explanation. The public outcry and anger against cadres and entrepreneurs who grew rich by privatising communal land were turning into a political force of strength that had torn down previous regimes. Public bitterness had to be carefully managed by protesters as well as the government in the joint interest of maintaining social stability. An analysis of messages posted on Local Leadership Message Boards between 2008 and 2014 shows that demands expressed by local citizens that were collective rather than individual, and were related to single issues and economic growth, were more likely to result in government response. The main concerns were related to agriculture, corruption, employment, and quality of services for businesses (Su & Meng, 2016). The return to Leninist governance tools, such as the extraction of public confessions, has also increased social control. Other social control mechanisms add to the risk of unsocial behaviour. Every Chinese person knows there is a government dossier on them and every village has a public "dossier" in the form of billboards that publish village statistics on matters like taxes, marriages, and abortions (Koss, 2018). Combined with this trend of increasing informal social control are increased disguised collective actions on the one hand and increased number of formal administrative lawsuits on the other (Fu, 2017; Fu & Diestelhorst, 2020). These mechanisms are no less effective in regulating rural enterprises and, in particular, their social impact and the government does not always have the upper hand.

## Religious communities

Disabilities and illness may be defined as a spiritual, medical, or social problem. In China today, medical explanations dominate. This, of course, has consequences for social enterprises, which define disabilities and illness as social constructs. In religious communities, on the other hand, they are understood in transcendental terms. Foucault's groundbreaking analyses of the redefinition of "madness" from a spiritual to a medical matter documents the vast institutional consequences of the difference (Foucault, 1988). In China today, any spirituality bordering on religion is problematic. In the CCP, religion equals superstition and "opium for the people." Religious communities were prohibited and dismantled in the Mao era, reappeared along with a strong religious revival in the Deng era, and have been disciplined and brought under increasingly firm control in the Xi era (Chang, 2020; Johnson, 2017; Yang, 2011). This in turn has direct consequences for religious communities' ability to address social needs.

Note that I use "religious community" as a general term for the huge variety of spiritual, religious, and transcendental communities, orders, and movements in China.

### *Religion in China*

Historically, religious communities in China addressed not only transcendental concerns, but health and social needs as well. Today, even in the urban areas, where advanced medical and social services are available, religious communities are still important for solace and support for worldly problems. Although the public health services in the remote, rural areas leave much to be desired, there are numerous local "barefoot" solutions, health clinics, homes, and advisory services alongside. Both traditional Chinese medicine and Western medicine is offered. Even though Chinese traditional medicine is different from Western medicine, and despite the heated debate as to its relative merit, it addresses medical problems, not spiritual ones. I emphasise this to make clear that the question if religious communities should and can offer medical services is not an issue here. The experiences are mixed. Some Christian missionaries active in China before the PRC was established offered treatment and care based on professional medical and nursing training, not religious teachings. In other cases, adherence to the specific religious belief of a community or order offering treatment was a condition for receiving treatment. Comparatively speaking, this is similar to managers using social benefits as mechanisms to incentivise or punish their workers. In China, as in other countries, transactional approaches to care are disputed (Chang, 2020; Mol, 2008). The purpose of the exploration here is to show how religious communities meet social, not medical needs.

The CCP is expressly secular, requesting atheism of its members. Religious communities may be sites for organising collective action and are therefore closely monitored. There is no freedom of religious expression. Organised religion is either heavily regulated or outright forbidden. National Islamic, Taoist, Buddhist, Roman Catholic, and Protestant religious associations are acknowledged by the government, and Buddhism and Taoism have been hailed as model religions (Chang, 2020). There has also been a government-supported revival of Confucianism since the 1990s (Goldman, 1986, 2002). The Roman Catholic Church is engaging with the idea of accepting that the CCP anoints bishops in China, and the diverse Protestant churches are well represented in the national governance bodies. Estimates are that around 20% or 300 million people are devoted Buddhists. At the other end of the scale are the dozen or so banned churches or movements. The popular mediation movement Falun Gong that combines Buddhist and Taoist principles with qigong practice is the best known of the recent movements.[3] Historically, forceful religious movements, like the Boxer movement and the Taiping Heavenly Kingdom, have been a threat to the political establishment. In the history of China, such movements are recognised to herald the end of dynasties and the CCP closely monitors any that may indicate similar forces at work (Fairbank & Goldman, 2006). In the early years of the communist movement, the revolutionaries opposed what they saw as local superstitions, cementing the powers of secret brotherhoods and local gentry

The majority of the population can be placed somewhere between the official religions and the banned ones. Estimates vary that between 20% and 75% of the population adhere to some form of "folk religion" or daily ritual observances. "Folk religion" is a loose term for a variety of belief systems, which in China may very well be a mix of several of the organised religions, in particular Buddhism, Taoism, and ancestral worship, often associated with Confucianism and filial piety towards the ancestors.

Regardless of the exact number, the majority of believers worship outside the officially accepted associations and sites and in numerous informal ways (Johnson, 2017). Underground house churches, that is, celebrations in private homes, and religious sites flourish (Fish, 2016). In private, there is a blurred line between the government and the people. Like the case discussed in chapter 4, about the Party secretary who donated a full set of Buddhist scriptures to the Academy, people move between the political and the religious domains and it works as long as no one makes too much of an issue about it. The number of Christians is estimated to be around 70 million and Muslims around 25 million, including people from ten of the ethnic minorities. In terms of monks and nuns, rabbis, priests, and imams, the number of clerics responsible for the management of religious institutions is far smaller and difficult to assess. To sum up, there has been a strong religious revival in China and religious communities have considerable influence on the social contract between the state and society.

### *The Jing'an temple episode*

The Jing'an Temple in downtown Shanghai is a monumental, gilded complex at the end of a high-end shopping area. In front of it is a small park, with abundant shrubbery and flowerbeds, small ponds and graceful willows, among which the locals stroll, chat, and exercise. At a seminar, a non-Shanghainese manager who had come to town for work derogatorily called it a government showpiece. She said it had cost millions of yuan to renovate but the investment had paid off as the temple now attracted only wealthy tourists. For religious services, she said, people would go to one of the informal churches. When I asked where I could find them, she shrugged and said that it depended on the need, I should look in the back streets, or find someone to introduce me. She then started to talk about something else. In the months following, I passed the golden temple on my way to work every day. It did look like an artificial showpiece but I saw a steady stream of people going in and out of it, even during winter when there were few tourists.

On a quiet winter day, I braved the expected inauthenticity and bought a ticket. It cost 50 yuan, which was expensive as temples go. The temple complex is huge quadrant, oriented roughly south-north. The west, north, and south outer walls are dotted with small stores selling religious paraphernalia. On the south wall are three large double doors with a classic pair of lions in front. On top of the wall are three pagoda-like golden structures. The only public entrance is a small door between the ticket office and the main doors. It opens into a large open-air courtyard. Three-storey buildings enclose the courtyard. In the middle is the main temple, so large that it even dwarfs the monumental incense burner at the foot of the stairs. The main hall is accessible by a wide central staircase and covered walkways lead to the eastern and western eaves. In contrast with the intricate, painted carvings on the outside, the main hall is nearly bare of decorations save a large, gilded Buddha and enormous wooden roof beams. On my first visit, a local noticed my interest in the beams and whispered that they were cut from sacred trees brought down from Myanmar. There were few offerings of any kind, no incense sticks burning, and no rattle of I Ching sticks that I was used to from Chinese temples elsewhere. The whole complex was monumental and majestic, indeed a showpiece.

Yet, there was peace in the place not often found in the bustle of Shanghai. I returned time and again for the sense of freedom and open space. The building behind the main hall and part of the eastern eaves contained inaccessible living and working quarters. The rest of the complex contained several smaller halls with altars, including one for the goddess of mercy, Guanyin, and a jade and a silver Buddha. Other religious paraphernalia were displayed in the south wall pagodas. On the ground floor were meeting rooms, technical rooms, a kitchen and a dining area.

Once a door to a hall in the western building stood open. Inside I could see an ancestral hall containing rows of ancestral tablets. People were making offerings. In Southeast Asia, people who do not have descendants or who fear that their descendants will not care for them in their afterlife can pay a temple to do the required regular offerings. People who do not have access to an ancestral hall may also acquire a place for a tablet in a temple. However, it was quite surprising to find such a place in this supposedly artificial showpiece of a temple.

One day there were more people hanging around in the courtyard than usual. I was in the main hall, relishing the peace, when a train of singing monks approached. They entered through the huge main entrance and began a celebration in front of the altar. I could not leave the room without getting in the way, so waited in a corner. People poured in until every corner of the room filled up with devotees, chanting, bowing in rhythm with the monks' prayers. I knew enough of the ritual proceedings to pay my respects along with the devotees, and simply moved along in the line towards the altar and then out the side door. The only Caucasian in the room and packed together with the mass of people, no one stared at me or pointed, as happened regularly on the metro or other places where the locals did not expect foreigners. People were engaging in prayer and celebration of the ritual and not in judging others.

Outside, other devotees who had received their blessings waited until the monks exited the main hall in a procession. They crossed the walkway to the eastern building and continued south. The yellow-robed figures, more than 50 as far as I could count, were followed by a large number of black-clad nuns. More and more monks and nuns appeared. Now there was a procession from the western halls as well. The processions congregated by the south hall, with devotees filling every available space close to them. It was barely possible for me to get down by the main stairs. With chants, gongs, and cymbals ringing in my ears, I crossed the courtyard, now filled with the smell of incense from the lighted sticks held by the devotees. There had not been anything artificial about this celebration. These contradictory impressions from the Jing'an temple illustrate the status of religious life in China. Religion is allowed because it is good for spiritual wellbeing and adds to economic development, but only if discreet and disciplined.

### *Faith-based social service providers*

In response to the strict government control on organised religion, religious beliefs have found expressions in many other channels, such as health, education, medicine, tourism, heritage, and ethnic minority activities (Palmer, 2009), as well as poverty reduction initiatives (Carino, 2016). There are also a large number of explicitly religious non-governmental organisations (RNGO). They are described as "some of the most resilient social organisations outside the party-state structure" (Tam & Hasmath, 2015, p. 284). A number of faith-based organisations have the provision of social services as their social mission. A recent study found three main types: Established orders that hire social workers, social organisations supported by religious bodies, and social organisations operated by religious social workers, not attached to any organised religion (Xu, 2020). Although all types of organisations to some extent receive funding from the government, the third type has the most diverse funding sources, highest trust among its stakeholders and operates the most independently of the government.

The purpose of Xu's study was to identify the best placement site for social work students and interestingly concludes that students get the best opportunity to critically reflect on their values and ethical stance in the third type of organisation. This is the most complex type of organisation with the most stakeholders. Like the social enterprise, it succeeds because it manages to fill the different positions required to mobilise resources from a variety of stakeholders. A prominent example of the first type of faith-based association, and one that balances close relations with the central government and local social services, is the charity Protestant Amity Foundation (Carino, 2016). It was established in 1985 with the purpose of helping foreign English teachers and supplying Chinese Christians with Bibles through its printing press (amityfoundation.org). Over the years it has expanded its services to elderly care, orphanages, help centres for people with autism and mental problems, as well as special education institutions. One of its founders, Bishop K.H. Ting, was a vice-chairman of the Chinese People's Political Consultative Conference and a member of the National People's Congress. The foundation also maintains close relations with international organisations and donors.

An example of the second type of faith-based organisation is the traditional temple. The landscape of China is dotted with temples and, like the SOEs, they are similar to functional towns. "To the resident monks and nuns, a temple is more than a religious space: it provides all their social and material necessities, including education, shelter, livelihood, healthcare and old-age care" (Chang, 2020, p. 447). For elderly people without descendants to take care of them, joining a temple used to be a possibility before the Mao era (Dikötter, 2010, p. 264).

Although limited in numbers, the traditional temple shows another side of the religious organisation as social service provider. Since the Opening Up reforms, religious bodies have gradually been allowed to resurface. Two conflicting forces have shaped the process. First, the re-emergence of the religious association was not for the sake of religious freedom, but to give the government a better overview and control (Goldman, 1986). Second, in line with market economy principles, since religious activity is not defined as productive and worth investing in, all restoration costs had to be borne by the religious bodies themselves (Chang, 2020).

Restoration of temples and orders has been a daunting task. While religious orders were repressed in the first decades of the PRC, during the Cultural Revolution all religious sites were closed and many physically wrecked. Monks and nuns were imprisoned or forced to return to secular life. The reconstruction placed strong demands on the temple management. However, a number were able to attract funds from foreign donors. Others benefitted from the rapid economic growth that followed, by selling off land. As temple properties are communal, this required careful stakeholder management and produced the same kind of conflicts as those between villager and cadre in the secular parts of society. In other instances, the requirements for succeeding in the Han-dominated market economy conflicts with the transcendental personal and communal expectation of clerics among the ethnic minorities (Casas, 2016). Another opportunity has opened up through tourism, causing the temples to become more like businesses with entrance fees and gift shops.

The religious commodification is ironically known as "religion building a stage to sing an economic opera" (Chang 2020, p. 441). Although some temple leaders protested against religious symbols being used as trademarks, others have embraced the possibility to strengthen the temple by strengthening its economy. In this instance, the for-profit and the social, or rather transcendental, mission of the temples came into direct conflict, much more so than with the social enterprises. Adding to the complexity is the local government's interest in getting their share of the temples' income. The claim is that they are responsible for providing the necessary infrastructure that gets tourists to the sites and therefore must get their share of the rent. Another study points to different degrees of marketization of religion under communist rule (Yang, 2011).

The third type of faith-based organization is exemplified by the Sunshine Ecovillage. Established in 2015, it is a recent addition to the already diverse landscape of faith-based care-giving associations (ecovillage.org/project/sunshine-ecovillage-network) and bases its activities on Taoist principles by combining care for nature, education, and community. It offers ecological education and experiences in communal care for the environment to a limited number of adults and children. Part of the international eco-village and "education for sustainable development" movement, the village is located just outside Hangzhou, a town in the Zhejiang province and a popular destination for eco-tourists. Historically Hangzhou has been known for its natural beauty and the tranquillity of its lakes. The Sunshine Ecovillage combines new expressions of environmental and social concerns, through the sustainability discourse, with the age-old Daoist practise of retreating to nature.

Several researchers have noted that the former leading roles played by intellectuals and clergy radically changed during the Opening Up reforms. While formerly they were subservient to, but independent of, the state, they have either been co-opted as advisors to the government; as academics and analysts providing state-of-the-art analyses; as model figures in the national voluntary associations; or gone into business, entertainment or the media (Casas, 2016; Goldman, 2002; Polly, 2007). As with the rural movements, the trend is rightful resistance, especially with the young adults ((Fish, 2016). The Xi era policies of re-sinification and re-ideologisation can be regarded as a countermovement to the hollowing out of spiritual life, by mobilising intellectuals and believers, as well as a move to control this still largely unregulated part of society. Either way, faith-based associations play their part in redefining the social contract.

## Summing up

Even though not social enterprises as defined here, three types of enterprises and associations were and are important providers of social services in China: SOEs, rural cooperative economic organisations, and religious communities. As with the typical social enterprises, the atypical ones prove that the CCP is not alone in defining the content of the social contract. On the contrary, the influence goes both ways. The productivist approach is clearly recognisable in all instances, even in the management of temples. The quest for economic development goes hand in hand with dealing with social problems, both in the narrow sense of social work and the broad sense of maintaining "stability and harmony." The enterprises are busy taking care of their business and their various stakeholders. The social contract is as influenced by this as by pre-conceived government policies.

## Notes

1 China Statistical Yearbook, 2019. Table 1.8. Number of business entities by Region and Status of Registration. http://www.stats.gov.cn/tjsj/ndsj/2019/indexeh.htm
2 http://english.www.gov.cn/statecouncil/ministries/202101/13/content_WS5ffef541c6d0f72576943c9e.html.
3 Albert, 2015, Council on Foreign Relations, "CFR Backgrounders: Religion in China," June 10, 2015 | US-China Institute. https://china.usc.edu/council-foreign-relations-cfr-backgrounders-religion-china-june-10-2015.

## References


Bai, C.-E., Li, D. D., Tao, Z., & Wang, Y. (2000). A multitask theory of state enterprise reform. *Journal of Comparative Economics*, *28*(4), 716–738. https://doi.org/10.1006/jcec.2000.1681.

Brandtstädter, S. (2020). Rising from the ordinary: Virtue, the justice motif and moral change. *Anthropological Theory*, 146349962093205. https://doi.org/10.1177/1463499620932058.

Butcher, J. G. (1983). The demise of the revenue farm system in the federated Malay states. *Journal of Public Policy*, *17*(3), 387–412. https://doi.org/10.1017/S0143814X00003627.

Cao, X. (2017). Corporate social responsibility. In Q. Jiang, Qian Lixian, & D. Min (Eds.), *Fair development in China* (pp. 119–134). Springer.

Carino, T. C. (2016). Faith-based organisations between service delivery and social change in contemporary China: The experience of Amity Foundation. *HTS Teologiese Studies / Theological Studies*, *72*(4). https://doi.org/10.4102/hts.v72i4.3504.

Casas, R. (2016). The 'Khanan Dream': Engagements of former Buddhist Monks with the market economy in Sipsong Panna, PR China. *The Asia Pacific Journal of Anthropology*, *17*(2), 157–175. https://doi.org/10.1080/14442213.2016.1144077.

Chang, K.-m. (2020). Between spiritual economy and religious commodification: Negotiating temple autonomy in contemporary China. *The China Quarterly*, *242*, 440–459. https://doi.org/10.1017/S030574101900122X.

Che, J., & Qian, Y. (1998). Institutional environment, community government, and corporate governance: Understanding China's township-village enterprises. *Journal of Law, Economics, and Organization*, *14*(1), 1–23.

Cui, M., Pan, S. L., Newell, S., & Cui, L. (2017). Strategy, resource orchestration and e-commerce enabled social innovation in rural China. *The Journal of Strategic Information Systems*, *26*(1), 3–21. https://doi.org/10.1016/j.jsis.2016.10.001.

Dai, S., Wang, Y., & Liu, Y. (2019). The emergence of Chinese entrepreneurs: Social connections and innovation. *Journal of Entrepreneurship in Emerging Economies*, *11*(3), 351–368. https://doi.org/10.1108/JEEE-02-2018-0021.

Dikötter, F. (2010). *The tragedy of liberation: a history of the Chinese revolution, 1945-1957* (First U.S. Edition ed.). Bloomsbury Press.

Elfstrom, M. (2020). Holding the government's attention: State sector workers in China. In K. J. Koesel, V. J. Bunse, & J. C. Weiss (Eds.), *Citizens and the State in Authoritarian Regimes: Comparing China and Russia* (pp. 191–220). Oxford University Press.

Fairbank, J. K., & Goldman, M. (2006). *China: A new history* (2nd enl. ed.). Belknap Press of Harvard University Press.

Fish, E. (2016). China's millenials. *The want generation*. Rowman & Littlefield.

Foucault, M. (Ed.). (1988). *Madness and civilization: A history of insanity in the age of reason* (Vintage Books Ed., Nov. 1988 ed.). Random House.

Fu, D. (2017). Disguised collective action in China. *Comparative Political Studies*, *50*(4), 499–527. https://doi.org/10.1177/0010414015626437

Fu, D., & Diestelhorst, G. (2020). Political opportunities for participation and China's leadership transition. In K. J. Koesel, V. Bunce, & J. C. Weiss (Eds.), *Citizens and the state in authoritarian regimes: comparing China and Russia* (pp. 59–75). Oxford University Press.

Goldman, M. (1986). Religion in post-Mao China. *The Annals of the American Academy of Political and Social Science*, *483*, 146–156.

Goldman, M. (2002). A new relationship between the intellectuals and the state in the post-Mao period. In M. Goldman & L. O.-f. Lee (Eds.), *An intellectual history of modern China* (pp. 499–538). Cambridge University Press.

Gong, X., & Cortese, C. (2017). A socialist market economy with Chinese characteristics: The accounting annual report of China Mobile. *Accounting Forum*, *41*(3), 206–220. https://doi.org/10.1016/j.accfor.2017.04.002.

Johnson, I. (2017). *The souls of China: The return of religion after Mao*. Pantheon Books.

Koss, D. (2018). *Where the party rules: the rank and file of China's communist state*. Cambridge University Press.

Kung, J. K.-s., & Lin, Y.-m. (2007). The decline of township-and-village enterprises in China's economic transition. *World Development*, *35*(4), 569–584. https://doi.org/10.1016/j.worlddev.2006.06.004.

Li, X., & Soobaroyen, T. (2021). Accounting, ideological and political work and Chinese multinational operations: A neo-Gramscian perspective. *Critical Perspectives on Accounting*, *74*, 102160. https://doi.org/10.1016/j.cpa.2020.102160.

Li, Y., Fan, P., & Liu, Y. (2019). What makes better village development in traditional agricultural areas of China? Evidence from long-term observation of typical villages. *Habitat International*, *83*, 111–124. https://doi.org/10.1016/j.habitatint.2018.11.006.

Lin, J. G. L., & Xie, Y. (2018). *A century of change in a Chinese village: The crisis of the countryside*. Rowman & LIttlefield.

Lin, K. J., Lu, X., Zhang, J., & Zheng, Y. (2020). State-owned enterprises in China: A review of 40 years of research and practice. *China Journal of Accounting Research*, *13*(1), 31–55. https://doi.org/10.1016/j.cjar.2019.12.001.

Mao, Z. (1965). *Report on an Investigation of the Peasant Movement in Hunan*. Foreign Languages Press, 2nd ed.

McMillan, J., & Woodruff, C. (2002). The central role of entrepreneurs in transition economies. *Journal of Economic Perspectives*, *16*(3), 153–170. https://doi.org/10.1257/089533002760278767.

Mol, A. (2008). *The logic of care: Health and the problem of patient choice*. Routledge.

Mulvenon, J. C. (2000). *Soldiers of fortune. The rise and fall of the Chinese business-military complex 1978-1998*. Routledge.

O'Brien, K. J., & Li, L. (2006). *Rightful resistance in rural China*. Cambridge University Press. https://doi.org/10.1017/CBO9780511791086.

Palmer, D. A. (2009). China's Religious Danwei. Institutionalising Religion in the People's Republic. *China Perspectives*, *2009*(2009/4). https://doi.org/10.4000/chinaperspectives.4918.

Pan, Y. (2017). *Rural welfare in China*. Springer International Publishing: Imprint: Springer.

Park, A., & Sehrt, K. (2001). Tests of financial intermediation and banking reform in China. *Journal of Comparative Economics*, *29*(4), 608–644. https://doi.org/10.1006/jcec.2001.1740.

Park, A., & Shen, M. (2003). Joint liability lending and the rise and fall of China's township and village enterprises. *Journal of Development Economics*, *71*(2), 497–531. https://doi.org/10.1016/S0304-3878(03)00038-5.

Patnaik, U. (1987). Three communes and a production brigade: The contract responsibility system in China. *Social Scientist*, *15*(11/12), 34–61. https://doi.org/10.2307/3520233.

Polanyi, K. (Ed.). (2001). *The great transformation: The political and economic origins of our time* (2nd Beacon Paperback ed.). Beacon Press.

Polly, M. (2007). *American Shaolin: Flying kicks, buddhist monks, and the legend of iron crotch: an odyssey in the new China*. Avery.

Su, Z., & Meng, T. (2016). Selective responsiveness: Online public demands and government responsiveness in authoritarian China. *Social Science Research*, *59*, 52–67. https://doi.org/10.1016/j.ssresearch.2016.04.017.

Tam, J., & Hasmath, R. (2015). *Navigating uncertainty: The survival strategies of religious NGOs in China. Journal of Civil Society*, *11*(3), 283–299. https://doi.org/10.1080/17448689.2015.1061261.

Wang, J. (2014). The political logic of corporate governance in China's state-owned enterprises. *Cornell International Law Journal*, *47*(3), 631–670.

Wei, Y. D., Lin, J., & Zhang, L. (2020). E-commerce, Taobao villages and regional development in China. *Geographical Review*, *110*(3), 380–405. https://doi.org/10.1111/gere.12367.

Whiting, S. H. (2000). *Power and wealth in rural China: The political economy of institutional change*. Cambridge University Press.

Wu, J., Zhuo, S. H., & Wu, Z. F. (2017). National innovation system, social entrepreneurship, and rural economic growth in China. *Technological Forecasting and Social Change*, *121*, 238–250. https://doi.org/10.1016/j.techfore.2016.10.014.

Xu, Y. (2020). Professionalism and Sustainability of Faith-based Social Work Organisations in China. *China: An International Journal*, *18*(4), 123–140.

Yang, F. (2011). *Religion in China: Survival and revival under communist rule*. Oxford University Press.

# Part III
# Discussion

# 7 How social enterprises alter the social contract

Social enterprises change the social contract by entering into various stakeholder positions, combining them into configurations of people, objects, and concepts. They occupy these positions to mobilise resources and gain legitimacy. The cases presented in some detail in previous chapters have all been in business for more than five years, the customary timeline that confirms whether a start-up has succeeded or not. This chapter discusses how they managed to balance the various positions, and thereby make ever so slight changes to the social contract. Before I discuss this more general topic, a consideration of three conditions that determine access to resources is in order. The three determinants are production factors, relative quality of the product or service offered, and the quality of social relations.

## The status of the production factors

The first requirement of any enterprise is access to the means of production, what Michael Porter, an acclaimed business strategy professor, defines as the factor conditions (Porter, 2008). The factors constitute the resource base of an enterprise and their conditions determine their availability and quality. According to neo-classic economic theory, the identified factor conditions are land, capital, and labour. Later research has identified other types of capital as well: Goodwill, intellectual property, and social capital. However, as capital accumulation per se is not the main theme here, I will not discuss these further.

Land is not a crucial production factor for most social enterprises. Neither are they particularly capital-intensive. Capital is crucial only insofar as it includes buildings, machinery/equipment, and funds needed to provide the social services. Acquiring a place to operate from is a first step in becoming recognised as a separate, dependable enterprise. Without a plant, a meeting place, a shop, and a museum there would be no sustainable business. In China, most social enterprises have usury rights to the capital, rather than ownership, which means they must carefully maintain relations with the owners of the capital.

DOI: 10.4324/9780429282591-7

When it comes to the three social enterprises analysed in detail in previous chapters, their access to capital varies. Only in the case of DEW is there a private owner. In the other cases, ownership is communal, which is more the norm in China. In terms of equipment, none of them acquires costly, technologically advanced equipment. The production machinery, books, and paper, and embroidery equipment is mostly donated or borrowed. Financial resources are needed to set up and run the enterprises but not to distribute profits to owners. The three enterprises finance their operations in various ways: Through sales, fees, and donations. None of them has access to the capital markets or direct access to foreign donations, except through the government. Generally, foreign donations are mainly garnered by the central government and "filtered" down to qualified, deserving units anyway (Spires et al., 2014). These social enterprises are all labour intensive. In fact, it is part of their social mission to provide work or work-like activities that enhance the productive capabilities of the beneficiaries. Therefore, labour costs are more akin to investments than expenses. As expenses, labour costs are significantly reduced, anyway, due to the contribution of volunteers. Developing a support system of volunteers is, therefore, also economically important for these social enterprises. The conditions of the factors of land, capital and labour require these social enterprises to carefully manage their relations, not only with the government, but with a range of other stakeholders.

## Can their products or services be copied?

In the Porterian thinking, maintaining market position depends on whether or not a product or service is easy to copy. If unique, or the cost of copying is high, then it is possible to maintain a dominant market position. This is a challenge for many social enterprises. Their services cannot be trademarked or patented. This makes them vulnerable to competitors. Adding to the difficulty is the fact that they are established to do good. If they have designed a business model that allows them to do so in a better or cheaper way than incumbent enterprises, it should be in their interest to freely share the business model with other stakeholders. The problem for owners and managers of social enterprises is that they get little or no return on the resources invested in developing the enterprise. This is a particular challenge for social enterprises in China due to the government's habit of using NGOs to try out innovative new practices and take over those that work (Farid, 2019) or extract rent (Huang, 2008). The learning approach in the Deng era was known as "crossing the river by feeling the stones," continued from the Mao era's "from point to surface" practice-based learning approach (Heilmann, 2008). Heilmann shows how government policies have oscillated between open-ended local experiments and centrally conceived and controlled models. The governmental acceptance of experimentation at any point in time is, therefore, part of the product conditions. If open for experimentation, successful ideas will likely be co-opted by the government, and if centrally determined, it is even harder to get support for a unique new idea. As the social enterprises' products and services are, and should be, easily accessible, and their economic surplus an addition to the public finances, they are in a vulnerable position. Adding to the problem is the "muddled middle" of the government hierarchy, with numerous examples that the extracted rent has been transferred to other private entrepreneurs, urban and rural, commercial and communal (Huang, 2008; Whiting, 2000).

Therefore, in terms of uniqueness of products and services, commercially scalable solutions may be copied not only by the government but also by commercial enterprises. As China's commercial laws are not well developed, social enterprises cannot depend on legal protection for their technologies or business models. Neither can commercial enterprises. In terms of uniqueness of their products and services, they are in a much more vulnerable position than government agencies, while in fierce competition with commercial enterprises, domestic or international. How then do relations management condition the product and service factors?

## Relational conditions

Michael Porter's research interest was spurred by the fact that some industries and nations did better economically than others (Porter, 1990, 1998, 2011). He identified four determinants that characterised successful industrial clusters. These determinants influence social industry as much as commerce and manufacture. Three of these four determinants are demand conditions (the situation in the home market); related and supporting industries (collaboration environment); firm structure, strategy, and rivalry; and factor conditions (discussed above).

In China, the CCP is an all-encompassing relational condition. For one thing, a high level of state and communal ownership of resources is an important condition for the accumulation of capital. Another is conditions in the Party and government hierarchies. In addition to co-optation and rent extraction, rapid turnover of local party officials limits the pay-off for establishing social relations with Party officials (Eaton & Kostka, 2014). Differences in officials' priorities also matter. One study differentiated between officials as innovators or implementors (Newland, 2018). Innovators seek to advance their careers by working with social organisations and are more attentive and supportive of the NGOs but also more interested in activities that support their career possibilities. Implementers have long-term views and worked to ensure stability and continuity, but are less interested in taking the risk of dealing with outsiders. They were harder to be acquainted with, but more stable in their support once gained. Another study found that NGOs could reduce the risk of working with government officials through collaborative effort among themselves to connect with government-backed national foundations, however, this is also a risky approach because the Party represses collective action outside the government (Li et al., 2016). Complicating the picture are the many variations in local governance practices, the muddled middle of the government hierarchy, and the aloofness of the central decision-making bodies.

The complexity, however, is also an important condition for social enterprises because it opens a wide space of opportunities. China works in the way that central communiques are operationalised as they are filtered down to the lowest level, while successful local good practices are floated upwards. In theory, it is supposed to be a recursive, learning system, and sometimes it is. The social enterprises that manage to establish reliable, working solutions have found this to their advantage.

## Socio-cultural configurations in the market

As defined in the introduction, a socio-cultural configuration is a number of organization-level social positions that mutually constitute each other. The configurations gain meaning from symbols that connect them with underlying ontological assumptions; in other words, the content of the social contract.

Every so often, an alien position appears within a configuration, or the meaning of a position is slightly changed. The changes must of necessity be slight. A foundational study in the field of innovation concluded, without doubt, that if an innovative, new practice is conceived as too different or incomprehensible, it will not attract followers (Rogers, 2003). Social entrepreneurs must therefore be able to fill existing positions in order to gain access to resources, recognition and legitimacy, but also to make changes to them to create space for the new enterprise. I now take a closer look at three typical configurations in the market and whether, when and how DEW, the Academy and the Institute altered positions within them.

## The commercial configuration

All markets, trade fairs, retail outlets, in short, any commerce is made up of customers and suppliers, and without merchandise and a price to predicate the movement of objects between them, it would not be possible to conceptualise market trading. This is why this configuration is labelled commercial. In Figure 7.1, this most basic market configuration is visualised.

The proto-economists who first developed economic theory borrowed concepts from real-life markets and modelled the economic models on market transactions. The particular concepts and modelling devices that make up economics have since come to gain a life of their own as universal representations of properties of human or systemic behaviour. The price

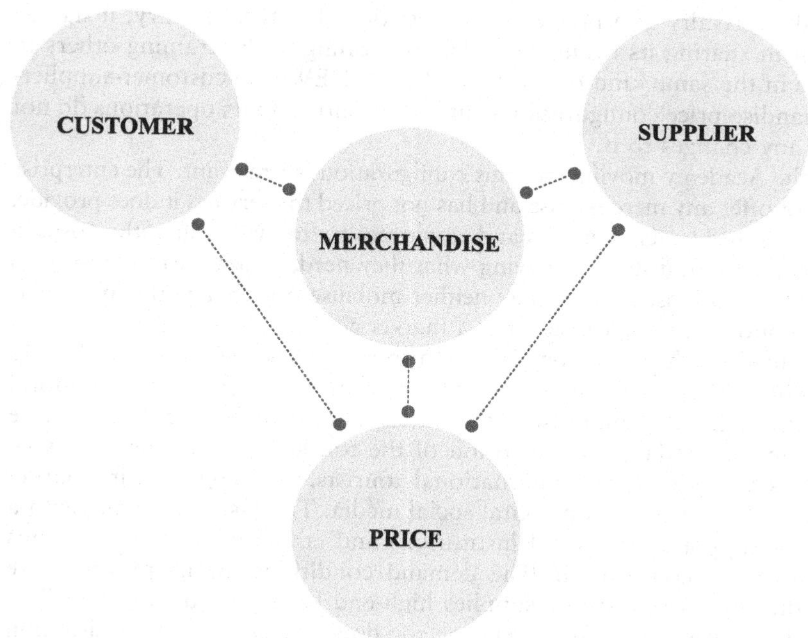


*Figure 7.1* The customer-supplier configuration.

mechanism is a key determinant in economic theory, and, therefore, a crucial element in any market mechanism. In one sense this is correct because all societies have markets, places for the exchange of goods and products. A classic anthropological study documents that even the existing Neolithic tribes practice trade (Sharp, 1952). How then do social enterprises in the various economic spheres fill this configuration, and how does this influence their access to resources?

DEW, which operates in the international market sphere, fits very well into the customer-supplier configuration. The enterprise is a supplier, within a special economic zone industrial cluster, and sells its products to other commercial actors. The conditions of its production factors are determined by its position within a multinational corporation. The corporation is further linked with a range of mutually supportive enterprises and organisations in China and abroad. The demand conditions are relatively predictable, after it has proved to be a trustworthy supplier of products of the right quality. The firm's strategy and structure has placed it in a position with little rivalry, so in a sense it holds a dominant market position within its chosen niche. DEW does not ask for special treatment in terms of product quality or supplies but operates fully as any commercial actor. Its products are quite easy to copy, being low-tech. The relational conditions are good. It is the brainchild of a range of stakeholders, which reduces the risk of rivalry and predatory competition. On the contrary, it has an interest in sharing its business model and scaling up by training others to engage in the same kind of social work. For DEW, the customer-supplier-merchandise-price configuration is unproblematic and its operations do not affect any changes to it.

To the Academy moving into this configuration is irrelevant. The enterprise does not offer any merchandise and has not priced the services it does provide. As far as possible, its managers and employees try to avoid filling the position of customer and, instead of buying what they need, acquire it in the form of gifts and donations. By this, they neither mobilise nor change this particular configuration. The enterprise is not a market actor.

The Institute has positioned itself firmly in the market sphere, but its positioning it actually steers resources from the market to the moral economy without demoralising the latter. The Institute is even an astute player in the predatory competition of the tourism industry as it sells its products to national and international tourists. It strengthens its market position by its presence on digital social media. The Institute's links with a range of supportive artisanal institutions and ethnic minority institutions mediate fierce competition. The demand conditions for its products are unpredictable. The Institute supplies high-end luxury products, as well as cheap souvenirs, and both depend on the flow of tourists. As the situation with the recent pandemic has shown, the flow can quickly dry up. As the enterprise has not yet established itself as a digital supplier, but depends on customers' physical presence, it has not yet been able to capitalise on new technology to innovate. This may be a function of its strategy and structure and lack of digitalised competition. Its market position is strengthened by the fact that neither the embroidery technique nor the design of its products are easy to copy. Even though there are a few rivals in the area, the products are priceless in their beauty and quality. In the case of the Institute then, the customer-supplier-merchandise-price configuration is unproblematic, and the enterprise does not affect any changes to it.

## The capitalist configuration

As important as buying and selling is in the market economy, is owning and managing. The object that discursively connects these positions are is capital and the predicate mechanism is, of course, profit. Figure 7.2 visualised the connections between the various positions in this configuration.

While the limited company form releases masses of private financial capital to be invested in new factories and plants, the large infrastructure projects that literally paved the way for industrialisation brought in the management hierarchies. No owner could oversee the whole construction site of a large railway project, so along came managers who supervised other managers. This was the beginning of the modern corporation and,

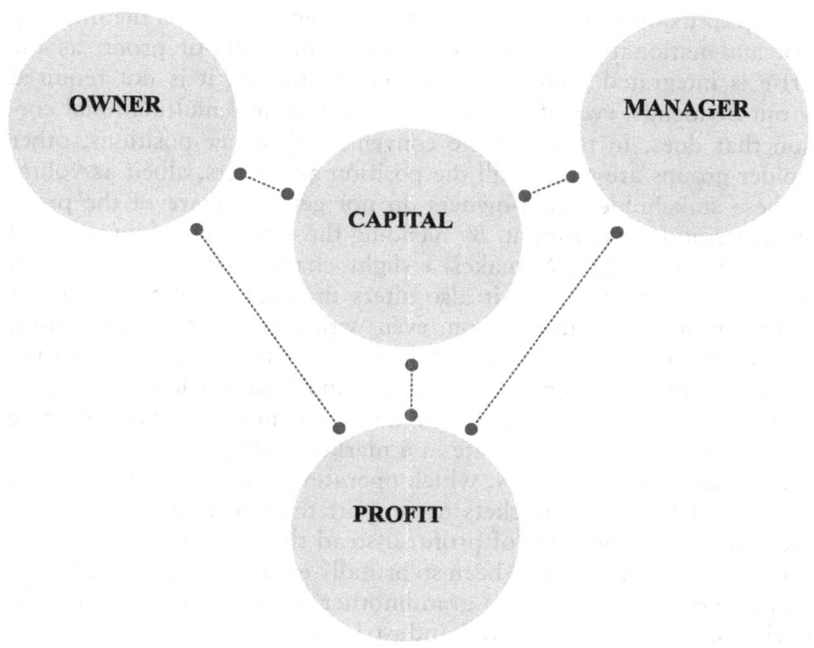


*Figure 7.2* The owner-manager configuration.

with it, the relations of production were forever changed (Chandler, 1993; Shannon, 1954). From these organisational innovations emerged the owner-manager-capital-profit configuration that dominates the political economies of today. Gone were the partnerships between people who took unlimited risks in a business venture. Gone was the owner-cum-manager who knew every detail of the business operations. Ownership of the means of production still made for clear social distinctions, but in a new form. Ownership of limited capital defined the relationship between the subject positions of owners and managers. The predicate position of profit still brings owners and managers clearly into view in the problem of how to ensure that owners still get their fair share of the profit, when the managers have all the detailed knowledge of the operations, including the finances (Berle & Means, 1991). Since managers helped generate the profit, how much of it is their due? This is still a contentious issue in many corporations. It is not so in most social enterprises, where the invested capital is limited, but the positions are part of the everyday set up.

DEW, which operates in the international market economy, has positioned itself well within the owner–manager configuration. Its management structure is a standard corporation functional hierarchy, with one exception. People with specialised competence in supported employment are part of its top management team. The relevant production factor, capital, is provided from its owners but also other stakeholders, such as the industry network and national voluntary associations. In terms of profit, as the enterprise is integrated with a management hierarchy, it is not required to pay out dividends, even if it is part of a professional multinational corporation that does. In terms of the conventional owner positions, other stakeholder groups are able to fill the position as owners, albeit as volunteers. These stakeholders-cum-owners do not get any share of the profit or compensation for their input. By blending the categories of owners and external stakeholders, DEW makes a slight change to the conventional owner–manager configuration. It also alters the content of the predicate profit. The set-up is not uncommon, even within commercial enterprises, and is done to connect with broader society, but it does break with the shareholder ideology of other corporations and business interest groups. DEW makes several small changes to this configuration, without going beyond what is culturally legitimate in a market setting.

The founders of the Academy, which operates in the modern economy, still pay out of their own pockets to support the operations but do not demand payback in the form of profit. Instead the sociocultural position of capitalist–owner, which had been so brutally eradicated in the Mao era, was made relevant again by the grandmother who gently claimed ownership rights, of sorts, to the old industrial factory building. Through this move, the enterprise gained access to a crucial production factor – buildings – by adding another position to the local social contract. The change was slight because the grandmother did not claim ownership in the sense of full control of the resource. Instead the claim was usury rights based on her family's former private ownership. In this instance, there was no alteration in the subject position of manager, so in a way, while the position of owner reappeared, the rest of the configuration did not. It worked in this context because of her personal social standing in the community. By that move, she influenced the resource conditions considerably. Having premises of its own, made it easier for the Academy to plan and offer a unique service and gave it prominence compared with other institutions that offered training and teaching on an ad hoc basis. Hence, the Academy made a slight change to the social contract by evoking a position that had been repressed for a long time. This made a big difference for the enterprise, without challenging the existing pattern of relations with the Party and the government.

The Institute, which operates in the moral economy, does not really position itself within the owner–manager configuration. For one thing, its managers are also independent artists. They share their intellectual capital and skills by transferring them to designs and embroidery techniques but maintain ownership of their individual artwork. Also, ownership of other means of production is communal and usury rights to land and buildings are obtained through connections with the ethnic minority as well as the government. Thus the enterprise did not activate the positions in this configuration and did not add new content.

## The worklife configuration

The relations between those who do the work tasks and those who plan and control is crucial in any economy. While subsumed under other social bonds in pre-modern economies, the positions got singled out and surfaced to prominence with industrialisation. The pattern of relationships that developed is still common today, despite the emergence of the gig economy and the increasingly common precarious work arrangements (Hepp et al., 2020). An employer provides work for the employee, who performs it and gets paid a wage (see Figure 7.3). The sharing of wages between employers and employees is as contentious an issue as the sharing of profit between owners and managers.

At DEW the position of employee is distinct from that of employer. DEW alters the content in the configuration by insisting that disabled workers are treated exactly like other workers. They must be paid fair salaries and have the same benefits. In this, the enterprise nuances the factor conditions of labour. Its founders cut straight to the heart of the conflict of interest between

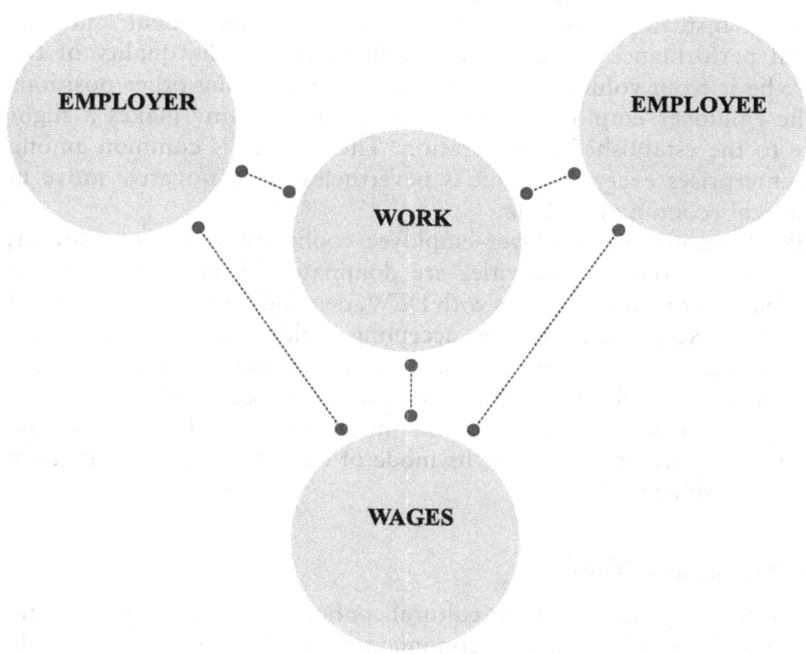


*Figure 7.3* The employer-employee configuration.

employers and employees over what wages should be paid for what type of work. The social entrepreneurs started an enterprise firmly on the side of the employees, without dissolving the category of employer. The product condition is that DEW produces an easily copied product but not easy-to-copy work conditions, as they have been specially adapted to the individual worker's needs. The enterprise claims that this adds little to investments but adds a lot to productivity. The demand for work is high but also hidden, which makes for somewhat contradictory demand conditions that the employer must sort out. In terms of its relational conditions, they also extend beyond that of the employee–employer configuration as the employers must occupy other positions vis-à-vis the families and villages of their workers. In all, DEW affected a number of small changes to the configuration.

At the Academy, the employees are also crucial for operations. Unemployment in the local community is high, especially among non-skilled workers, so the demand conditions are favourable for the employers. In line with the Academy's social mission, employers refrain from exploiting the situation by "buying" cheap labour. Although this would reduce operating costs, it would redefine the relationship with employees and turn it into a customer–supplier configuration. For the employers, having employees with a willingness to share and care for beneficiaries is more important. Unpaid work is done by volunteers, who may be recruited as employees if they perform well. In this the Academy makes a slight change to the configuration by connecting employee with that of volunteers. Instead of economic incentives, firm management and professional performance indicators are used to ensure the quality of the service, be it from volunteers or employees. By bringing other positions into the employer–employee configuration, the Academy makes a slight change to the established configuration. This change is common among social enterprises everywhere but is nevertheless an innovative move in the political economy of China.

At the Institute, the employer–employee configuration is not relevant, with one exception. The activities are dominated by an older artisanal master–bachelor relationship. As with DEW, demand for labour is high and hidden. The exception is that by accepting males and people with disabilities as students and potential teachers, the Institute alters the conceptions of who is employable where. Its operations secure the transfer of financial flows from the market to the moral economy. Likewise, by redefining the nature of employees, its mode of operation affects changes in all economic spheres.

## Marx, Lenin, and Mao

So far in this chapter, three socio-cultural configurations, and how they are activated differently in the three economic spheres, have been discussed. In practice, the configurations are often evoked simultaneously. This creates considerable tension, but of a different kind in China than in a Western market economy. It is, therefore, necessary to dig a bit deeper into the intellectual origins of these configurations, although it is not possible to give credit to the enormous body of literature that deals with them.

Economic theory was originally modelled on the pre-industrial market processes, where the category of employee, or worker, did not exist in the sense it is used today. There were disagreements among the proto-economists between those who thought that the value (and price) of goods should be calculated according to the expenditure of labour or according to how much someone was willing to pay for the product (of that labour). This is still an unresolved issue in economic theory, and it complicates industrial relations all over the world. Karl Marx brought the concept of labour firmly into economic models, thereby paving the way for an alternative understanding of markets and the capitalist economy (Marx, 1992). Marx distinguished between the worker and the work. A worker contracts an amount and quality of labour to an employer for a certain price. However, if the employer manages to increase productivity by organising the work more efficiently, or to leverage it with the aid of machines and technology, the increased earnings remain the property of the employer. Before workers organised, this economic logic resulted in the severe exploitation of workers who got no part of the increased profit. With the coming of the labour movement, the conflict was conceptualised as as a tension between state and society, not only capitalists and non-capitalists. In communist countries, the way to solve this conflict was revolution (Lenin, 2011). Other countries institutionalised Industrial Relations (Sejersted, 2011). The problem of the exploitation of workers is as acute today as in historical times, in particular where markets are not regulated. In market economies where unions and legal regulations are strong, the conflict of interest is worked out through regular collective agreements. In market economies where the unions and legal regulations are weak, there are individual negotiations, often based on established industry standards. In China the Leninist approach to the organisation of industrial relations is somewhat of a dilemma.

The nature of the social contract in China establishes particular conditions for the socio-cultural configurations. The employer–employee configuration is well established, while the two other configurations have been almost eradicated. The unions are strong and controlled by the Party. Both are supported by ideology, while the legal framework is weak, leaving much to be worked out in practice. In the Marxist communist paradise, workers were no longer alienated from the product of their labour and had even gained full control of all factors of production. The category of buyer and seller of labour, as well as owner and manager, were no longer needed. As this would not happen on its own, it was to be helped along by the revolution of the proletariat. The Leninist addition to this idea was that the proletariat was to be aided by an intellectual avant-garde that would govern the new society, to the extent that governance was needed. This Marxist-Leninist understanding informed the development of China's economy in the Mao era. Mao, however, found that in the rural economy of China, peasants by necessity needed to be mobilised, as the main force of the revolution, and to build up power in the villages in order to approach the cities from a position of strength in the countryside (Mao, 1965). After the proclamation of the PRC, revolution followed. Private property right was abolished, workers were controlled by the Party, capitalist land and industry owners and their families were killed or ostracised (Dikötter, 2010). Not until private enterprises were legalised in 2002, when private owners were allowed to become Party members, did the position of owner and, with it, managers, employers, and employees reappear as legitimate social categories in the domestic economy. This, however, has not brought significant deviations from the foundational ideology of the CCP, which is transferred to new generations through the Party schools. "The Communist Party remains to this day an organisation firmly anchored not only in Leninist organisational principles, but also in the Maoist tradition of campaign-style politics" (Pieke, 2009, p. 27).

The ideology and the Party's control limits the possibility for filling the sociocultural positions of the market, even after the introduction of market economy mechanisms. In any market economy, the configurations give meaning to different activities. Tension and conflicts arise when there is ambiguity about what particular position is relevant in a given situation. If a manager behaves as a customer towards employees, this easily creates resentment for feeling like they are treated as commodities. There is a huge difference between the "buying and selling" of labour to increase short-term profit and long-term investment in the wellbeing of employees. Employers, simultaneously, must keep in mind the position of manager. They must balance the relations with owners and their share of the profit of the company with consideration of employees and their share in the form of wages. Getting employees to accept lower wages or poorer working conditions means more resources for investments, dividends to the owners, or wages to the managers. Such tensions drive the relations in enterprises in the market economy. In China, with its Marxist-Leninist-Maoist heritage, the configurations are intertwined with other configurations, as the discussion in the following section shows.

## Sociocultural configurations unique to China or outside the market

Below, I draw three other configurations that are either unique to China or found outside the market and discuss how the case social enterprises manoeuvre in and between them.

## The Chinese configuration

Unique to China, the relationships in this configuration (shown in Figure 7.4) are important for connecting state and civil society. Any changes in this configuration, therefore, also imply alternations to the content of the social contract.

The majority of people in China are not engaged in government affairs, but in economic activities in villages and neighbourhoods, cities and industrialised zones. Even though urbanisation is increasing, the majority of the population lives in villages. The main factor of production is land, which is communally owned and irreplaceable. As a production factor, land can only be accessed through relations with the communal units that control its use. Individual households contract the right to farm the land and keep part of the rent. Legally, communal land cannot be sold by private individuals, but the legal framework is weak and largely based on custom. Only in the last two decades have substantial portions of former farmland been privatised, sold or leased to developers for property development. Urban and industrial development is implied by national innovation policies. However, the illicit privatisation of communal land is not. This has been among the main conflicts between local cadres and villagers. These conflicts have brought into view the intimate connection between villagers

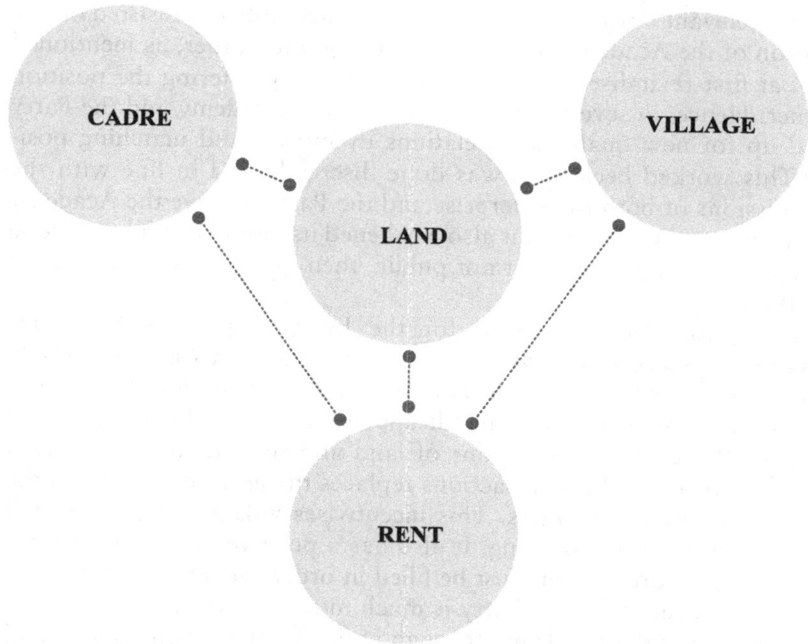


*Figure 7.4* The cadre-villager configuration.

and cadres. In relation to land, villagers, and cadres are mutually constitutive subject positions. Land is the source of rent, for the farmers who farm it, for the enterprises that operate on it, and the officials who tax them.

DEW enters this configuration only in order to recruit employees but cannot in any legitimate manner fill the complementary position of cadre. Cadres, however, serve as door openers to the villages for DEW employers. This brings the position of employer in from another configuration, especially in the recruitment process. DEW managers must engage with party cadres, both in the villages and the Gangshen SEZ, but cannot fill the position of villager. Land is not a production factor of any importance and DEW's operations do not depend on rent. As the position of manager mediates between that of villager and cadre, DEW opens new social space within the configuration without really altering it. This movement between and combining position connects the market and the modern economy. It requires considerable flexibility among all involved and may, in the long run, establish trust of the kind that does affect lasting social change. If that happens, a back door to modern industrial relations also opens for social enterprises in China.

As the activities of the Academy depend on the quality of their relations with party officials, this configuration is vital. All participants in the Academy's activities live either in the rural town or in the surrounding villages. They are therefore accustomed to entering the position of villagers. Although the Academy is not dependent on rent from land use, land became a relevant object position only when Party officials insisted on the relocation of the Academy to their land. The grandmother, as mentioned earlier, at first revitalised another configuration by entering the position of owner. Hence, in several small ways, both the Academy and the Party opened up for new qualities in relations by mixing and matching positions. This worked because it was done discreetly and in line with the social missions of both the enterprise and the Party. It gave the Academy access to resources. However, it also weakened its ability to offer a unique service as it became another, if not public, then quasi-public educational institution.

This configuration is relevant for the Institute as its student embroiderers are villagers and will return to their villages to set up shops or schools there in order to help develop the village economies of the Naxi, replaced ethnic minorities and handicapped youth. The Institute is only indirectly affected by the positions of land and rent. Its activities mean that income from market transactions replaces the need for rent from the land for some of the villagers. This incentivises village families to send their youth to town for training. It also has a positive impact on the position of Party cadre, which must be filled in order for the government to get its share of the rent. The Party is much more directly involved in this enterprise than in the Academy, through national innovation policies and the conventional governance mechanisms of model citizens. The Institute's activities also make it possible for its graduates to fill the position of villager and ethnic minority with new meaning. Now the Institute is an asset, which adds aesthetic and experiential value to the shopping. Hence, the Institute does affect slight changes to the configuration, although so far without generating any push-back from the government.

## The charity configuration

This configuration is typical of philanthropy all over the world but also relatively new. It is mediated by the boundary object impact. The configuration and can be visualised as shown in Figure 7.5.

Since the term social impact gained popularity in the first decades of the 2000s, a large body of rating institutions and financial instruments have appeared, making up the social impact arm of the financial industry. The object "social impact" changes the relationship between benefactors and beneficiaries, bringing the observable societal outcome to the front while backgrounding previous notions of altruistic motives of donors and (moral) failings of beneficiaries. It has also led to a redefinition of the meaning of grants as pure gifts, instead turning them into a source of investments, especially for social enterprises. This pattern is changing also in philanthropy in China. The configuration mirrors the Chinese

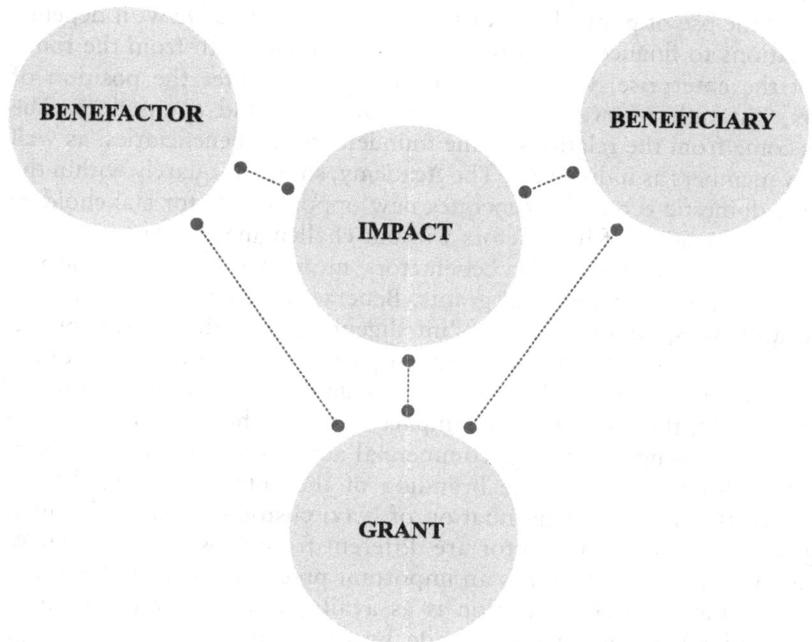


*Figure 7.5* The benefactor-beneficiary configuration.

patronage tradition. The patronages are neither as systemic as patron–client relationships in other parts of the world, nor as personal as *guanxi* networks. Patrons are elite figures in key positions and the reach of their patronage is only partly publicly known. The benefactor position mirrors that of patron. Grants from them come as much from the public coffers as from the wealth of private individuals or foundations.

For DEW, this configuration is relevant for its relations with foreign charities, which are represented on the board, and in its interest in developing services for the beneficiaries, the disabled workers. In this case foundations serve as "intelligent capital" but only supply "intelligence" and strengthen the Supported Employment approach of the managers, as well as helping to legitimise the approach vis-à-vis the rest of the industry cluster. The success of the enterprise is measured in terms of product quality and employee wellbeing, not broader social impact, and the enterprise does not fund its activities from grants but with income from the sale of products and, to some extent, public monies in the form of tax deductions. DEW makes changes to what the configuration means in China as cadre and owners also fill the position of benefactors. To some extent, this is merely a continuation of an established Chinese patronage practice but with the addition of foreigners.

For the Academy, the position of benefactor is crucial. The grandmother and the Party secretary clearly entered into this position in various ways. The social impact of the enterprise is carefully documented and used to legitimise the use of public land for its operations. Unlike DEW, it depends on donations to finance operations. The grants come both from the founders of the enterprise, who do not by that action enter the position of owners, but rather serve as benefactors, advisors, and counsellors. The grants come from the relations of the founders, of the beneficiaries, as well as Party members as individuals. The Academy, situated squarely within the modern, domestic economy, generates new opportunities for stakeholders to enter the position of benefactors without challenging the Party.

The Institute also depends on benefactors, more to acquire aesthetic and artisanal capital, than financial grants. Benefactors contribute with their talents and skills, another form of "intelligent" capital than that supplied by the benefactors of DEW, but as much part of the enterprise's resource base. The beneficiaries are the students who gain a means to make a living and, indirectly, their villages. The impact factor of the enterprise's activities is also a selling point in its commercial activities, as the aid to youth with disabilities is part of the branding of the enterprise. Equally important is its role in the continuation of Naxi customs. Hence, although the specifics of the impact factor are different from those for both DEW and the Academy, this factor is an important predicate position here too. In this instance, the configuration is as available in all three economic spheres and where the changes made by each enterprise indicate that this is a general effect on the social contract.

### *The civil society configuration*

This is the classic civil society configuration, the world of voluntary associations. Their key social position is the members. Members pay fees and elect their representatives. Fees are usually relatively limited sources of income for NGOs, while the representatives are crucial for strategic decision-making and connections with policymakers and regulators. In the club-like type of voluntary associations, substantial membership fees are required for membership, which again is a requirement to represent the organisation. In Figure 7.6, the interrelated positions appear.

For DEW, which operates in the market sphere, this configuration is nevertheless surprisingly relevant. Some of its board members serve as volunteers, and it bases its operations on a social mission, not according to a business model. The position of social mission also affects the noted changes to positions in other configurations, especially to the worker and benefactor positions.

For the Academy, this is a vital configuration because it is registered as a non-governmental organisation. However, it is not a classic voluntary association based on a congregation of like-minded members, who give up their spare time to realise a common social goal. Its membership base is the volunteers who organise the activities, and the families and teachers who

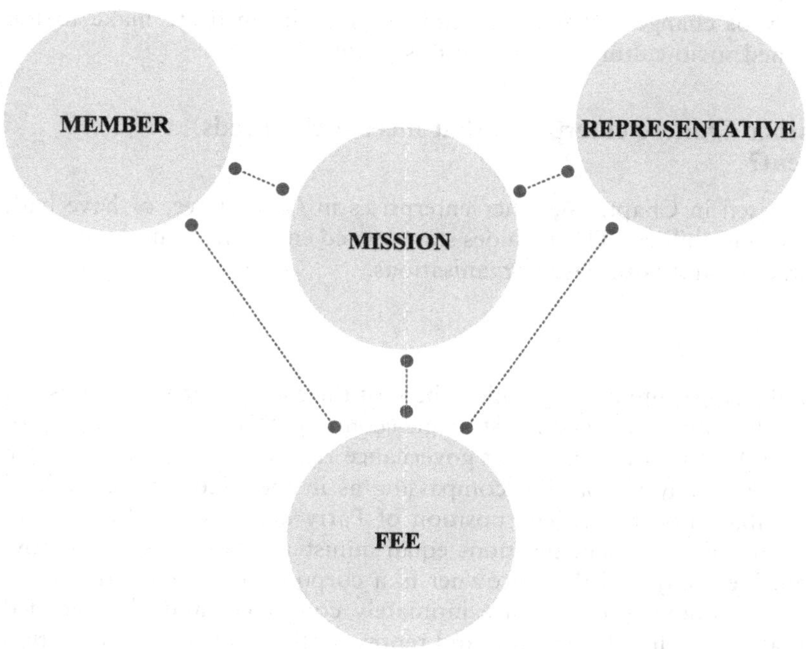


*Figure 7.6* The member-representative configuration.

make use of the Academy's services. In addition to the volunteers who donate their time, others connect with the Academy and contribute with gifts and donations. Donations are the sole source of income for the enterprise. Free labour, gifts and donations are forms of membership fees. The founders serve as the enterprise's representatives but are not elected in the classic fashion. Decision making happens through a systematic deliberation process between all stakeholders, much in the same way as members are engaged. The social mission is a powerful predicate that even mediates relations with the Party on those occasions when this configuration is brought to bear on a situation.

For the Institute, this configuration is not relevant, with one exception: Its social mission. It is neither a membership-based nor a club-like entity. It bases its operations on income and some grants, not fees. Its artisans also serve as master trainers and organise the numerous activities together with the students and their networks. Through all of its activities, the predicate of the social mission dominates. It requires great flexibility to manage the movement between subject and object positions of other configurations and still fill the social mission position.

## Summary of changes to the social contract

Social enterprises do not engage in the kind of social activism that conventional NGOs do but make social change in innovative ways. Here is a summary of changes DEW, the Academy and the Institute make to the established socio-cultural configurations (Table 7.1).

## Are other Chinese enterprises that meet social needs different?

As discussed in Chapter 6, other enterprises in China have, or have had, social responsibilities. This includes state owned enterprises, rural economic cooperatives and faith-based organisations.

### *SOEs*

The SOEs constitute an economic sphere of their own. For the purpose of brevity, this can be labelled the strategic economy. With the dismantling of smaller SOEs and the transfer of governance rights to the local levels, the strategic economy is not as encompassing as in the Mao era, but still of considerable importance. The position of Party cadre is equally relevant because top management positions equal ministerial positions in the government hierarchy and that of owner in a corporation. The cadre-owner-employer-customer positions are intimately connected, and also blended with that of supplier, benefactor, and representative. This is a continuation of the close connection between managers and employees and the Party

*Table 7.1* How the social enterprises changed the social contract

| | Configuration: | | | | | |
|---|---|---|---|---|---|---|
| *Social enterprise:* | *Commercial* | *Capitalist* | *Worklife* | *Chinese* | *Charity* | *Civil society* |
| DEW | No change | **Benefactors appear, redefined manager** | **Redefined employee and work** | **Foreign managers appear** | Not relevant | Not relevant |
| The Academy | Not relevant | **Redefined capital** | No change | **Owner appeared. Mission appered** | **Redefined impact** | No change |
| The Institute | No change | **Redefined profit** | **Redefined work** | **Redefined cadre** | **Redefined beneficiary** | Not relevant |

apparatus in the Mao era, and because of the current strategic role of SOEs as spearheads of China's economic growth, at home and abroad. These positions are mainly matched by those of employee and supplier (of labour). The SOEs are still manifestations of a communist economic system. According to productivist ideology, SOEs support welfare by providing the government with rent, in the form of taxes, and fees. That, of course, depends on how the government puts the surplus to use. The SOEs also employ about 60 million workers, which is far less than in their heyday, and is a measure of their reduced influence.

Some positions are not formally relevant, such as that of villager, because the SOEs are defined as urban units; likewise, that of beneficiary because benefits are part of wage packages. Other positions have a different loading. For example, the position of member is relevant in connection with membership of the CCP and may be mobilised by both employees and employers for internal Party deliberations. Due to the strategic importance of SOEs, the position of member may provide better access to resources than in the case of the social enterprises.

In terms of meeting social needs, SOEs are clearly not engaged because the object positions of impact and social mission are not relevant. Due to the hegemonic role of the state, this means that the state defines itself out of the social contract, which is an enormous change. In short, Chinese SOEs are actively engaged in altering the social contract but not in a way that is meant to enhance their capacity for meeting social needs. Regulation of the strategic economic sphere does not allow for transfer to other spheres.

### *Rural economic cooperatives*

I use "rural economic cooperative" here as a gloss for a range of rural economic initiatives, commercial and non-commercial. Various types of rural economic ventures have been organised in China's countryside. For some decades, economic activity was the privilege of the people's communes, brigades, and teams. Then the Town and Village Enterprises appeared, along with a mix of privately and publicly owned enterprises. The government is the major owner of all sources of capital, however, at the unruly village level there is communal ownership of land. This is why the villager-cadre-land-rent configuration is key and why it constitutes an economic sphere of its own. I call this the local economy. The rural economic cooperatives organise production, but the employer–employee configuration is less important than in the case of SOEs. The cooperatives also frequently enter the customer–supplier configuration, as they organise the sale of products on the open market. In other cases, the cooperative is started to provide a service that is too expensive for a single household or village to set up on its own. The benefactor–beneficiary and member–representative configurations are relevant because, in many instances, the cooperatives finance local social services for the elderly, health, and schooling. They are therefore actively engaged in realising social missions and social impact. To sum up, rural economic cooperatives are striving to do what they have always done. Here the connection between labour and the labourer is not severed, as in capitalist production, and the market is a place, not a principle. This means that the rural entities do not significantly alter the social contract.

### *Religious communities*

Religious communities include faith-based non-governmental organisations, as well as temples, churches, monasteries, mosques, and faith-based institutions. These communities still do their fair share of social work in China. They occupy a precarious position as they offer an alternative to the CCP dream – the communist paradise – only theirs is a transcendental state, while the communist paradise is of this world. I therefore call the faith-based organisations' part of the political economy the transcendental economy, Religious life in China is a syncretistic and tolerant affair in stark contrast with the harsh dogma of the CCP. Religious persecution is as aggressive as political persecution. Engagement in the provision of faith-based social services work therefore requires careful relationship management. The benefactor–beneficiary configuration is the most important and operations are usually mainly funded by grants and donations, which again require that the impact be accounted for.

Most important of all, however, is the social mission. This is undisputed but, unlike social enterprises, there is also a transcendental content to faith-based organisations. The mission serves as a powerful predicate position, more so than in any other of the economic spheres, and it is sustained by belief and trust in the spiritual realm. The members are devotees, and the representatives do not only represent the members but also other beings or spheres of existence. Hence the positions of member and representative are considerably expanded. As faith-based organisations are required to be well connected with the government, the cadre position is another key position. The beneficiaries of faith-based organisations are, in many cases, also villagers. Where the temple is a local affair, the usual configuration of villager–cadre may be mobilised but this requires careful manoeuvering on the part of the cadre. Faith-based organisations with foreign connections may fill the position of representative as a mediating position in the villager–cadre configuration. Land and buildings are important resources. They are accessible either through government connections, the market or donated by members of the congregations. This means that the customer–supplier configuration is also relevant in order to acquire income from the sale of products and experiences to devotees, as well as to tourists. This requires a careful balance between profit and social mission of the kind well known to social enterprises all over the world. Like social enterprises generally, faith-based organisations succeed because they manage to fill the different positions required to mobilise resources from a variety of stakeholders. In this they transgress boundaries between the spheres but, due to the Chinese government's stand against religion, they are not defined as parties to the social contract.

## Summing up

Three of the sociocultural configurations of the market are classic figures, but are brought to life in the moral and modern economic spheres as well. Managing the tensions that appear when positions of the various configurations overlap is part of everyday routine in market economies. This is not the case with the other three, which are either unique to China or outside the market. Like the literature about the market, there is a vast body of literature on the various aspects of state and civil society and the tensions and contradictions between them. As the discussion of the six sociocultural configurations has revealed, the distinction between the state, market and civil society is not particularly useful when it comes to China because the ideas about what belongs where is considerably different. Finding out precisely where to draw the lines is a recurrent issue in Chinese statecraft. In a sense, this is part of what makes China, China.

There are clear differences in how various types of enterprises fill the different sociocultural configurations and the kinds of changes this makes to the social contract. In the case of the social enterprises discussed, this is due to their way of working across the boundaries of economic spheres. They affect ever-so-slight changes to the configurations and thereby change the social contract. DEW paves the way for new industrial relations through their Supported Employment approach. The Institute steers flows of resources from the market to the moral economy, much aided by the institutions in the modern economy. The Academy brings professional business managerial competence into the Party. The way other types of enterprises make changes to the social contract, or not, is more due to conditions in their spheres. SOEs fill and blend the positions in ways that indicate the state intends to withdraw from the social contract and hence make large changes to its content, at least in the urban setting. The rural economic cooperatives, on the other hand, do not make major changes to its content but continue the established mix of profit and care, cooperation, and competition that characterises rural China. The religious communities are not really part of the social contract as it is today. They balance on a much sharper knife-edge than all the other enterprises as they are seen as competitors of the CCP. Common to all, is that they have found ways to make changes to the social contract without generating government pushback. What they do is a form of rightful resistance, only in a very social non-political manner that is quite new in China. They create a new, distinct and distinctly different Chinese society.

## References


Berle, A. A., & Means, G. C. (Eds.). (1991). *The modern corporation and private property* (2nd ed.). Transaction Publishers.

Chandler, A. D. (1993). *The visible hand: The managerial revolution in American Business*. Belknap Press of Harvard University Press.

Dikötter, F. (2010). *The tragedy of liberation: A history of the Chinese revolution, 1945–1957* (First U.S. ed.). Bloomsbury Press.

Eaton, S., & Kostka, G. (2014). Authoritarian environmentalism undermined? Local leaders' time horizons and environmental policy implementation in China. *The China Quarterly, 218*, 359–380. https://doi.org/10.1017/S0305741014000356

Farid, M. (2019). Advocacy in action: China's grassroots NGOs as catalysts for policy innovation. *Studies in Comparative International Development, 36*(4), 528–549. https://doi.org/10.1007/s12116-019-09292-3

Heilmann, S. (2008). From local experiments to national policy: The origins of China's distinctive policy process. *The China Journal, 59*, 1–30. https://doi.org/10.2307/20066378

Hepp, R.-D., Kergel, D., & Riesinger, R. (2020). *Precarized society: Social transformation of the welfare state* (1st ed., 2020.). Springer Fachmedien Wiesbaden: Imprint: Springer VS.

Huang, Y. (2008). Capitalism with Chinese characteristics. *Entrepreneurship and the state*. Cambridge University Press.

Lenin, V. I. (Ed.). (2011). *State and revolution*. Martino Publishing.

Li, H., Lo, C. W.-H., & Tang, S.-Y. (2016). Nonprofit policy advocacy under authoritarianism. *Public Administration Review, 77*(1), 103–117. https://doi.org/10.1111/puar.12585

Mao, Z. (1965). *Report on an investigation of the peasant movement in Hunan* (2nd ed.). Foreign Languages Press.

Marx, K. (Ed.). (1992). *Capital: Volume 1–3: A critique of political economy* (Vols. 1–3). Penguin Classics.

Newland, S. A. (2018). Innovators and implementers: The multilevel politics of civil society governance in rural China. *The China Quarterly, 233*, 22–42. https://doi.org/10.1017/S0305741017001734

Pieke, F. N. (2009). *The good communist: Elite training and state building in today's China*. Cambridge University Press.

Porter, M. (2008). The five competitive forces that shape strategy. *Harvard Business Review, 86*, 78-93, 137.

Porter, M. E. (1990). The competitive advantage of nations. *Harvard Business Review*. https://hbr.org/1990/03/the-competitive-advantage-of-nations

Porter, M. E. (1998). Clusters and the new economics of competition. *Harvard Business Review*. https://hbr.org/1998/11/clusters-and-the-new-economics-of-competition

Porter, M. E. (Ed.). (2011). *Competitive advantage of nations: Creating and sustaining superior performance*. Free Press.

Rogers, E. M. (Ed.). (2003). *Diffusion of innovations* (5th ed.) Free Press.

Sejersted, F. (2011). *The age of social democracy: Norway and Sweden in the twentieth century*. Princeton University Press.

Shannon, H. A. (1954). The coming of general limited liability. In E. M. Carus-Wilson (Ed.), *Essays in economic history* (Vol. 1, pp. 358– 339). E. Arnold.

Sharp, L. (1952). Steel axes for stone-age Australians. *Human Organization*, *11*(2), 17–22.

Spires, A. J., Tao, L., & Chan, K.-m. (2014). Societal support for China's grass-roots NGOs: Evidence from Yunnan, Guangdong and Beijing. *The China Journal*, *71*, 65–90. https://doi.org/10.1086/674554

Whiting, S. H. (2000). *Power and wealth in rural China: The political economy of institutional change*. Cambridge University Press.

# 8 How to engage in social entrepreneurship in China

In the introduction to this book, I cast light on two qualities of "social" in the missions of social enterprises in China. One is that it is better to be known as profit-minded than unsocial. The other is that civilised society springs from the quality of being. Without these qualities, the enterprises would not be recognisably *Chinese* social enterprises. However, these perceptions appear to run contrary to the dominant ideology, which is distinctly Chinese. Not only are the social enterprises discussed in this book practically successful, but they have also dealt successfully with fundamental cultural paradoxes. Seen in the light of these paradoxes, their achievements are remarkable. I will now take a closer look at these paradoxes.

## Civilised society and social engineering

Chapter 2 discussed the productivist national social innovation policies. The premise is that economic development equals social development. One conclusion following this premise is that rural entrepreneurship and Taobao villages enrich social life. The Academy, for its part, concluded that economic development made the town culturally poorer. The productivist premise allows for both conclusions but only the understanding added by the Academy includes civilised society.

Another example of this paradox is in the withdrawal of intellectuals and academics from public life. Intellectuals in the Mao and Deng eras contributed to China's development by sharing their independent thoughts. Many paid dearly for doing so but it was what the social contract demanded of true intellectuals. Prominent sinologists remark that in the Xi era the intellectuals no longer serve as intellectuals. Instead, they work in entertainment, business, or government research institutions. Here they contribute to economic development and social engineering. Do they contribute to civilised society? Are their choices social or unsocial?

The social enterprises discussed here do not contribute to the development of society in the manner of rural entrepreneurs or intellectuals. They are businesses set up to deal with practical everyday affairs, which aligns them directly with productivist beliefs. Yet their mission is to revitalise a

DOI: 10.4324/9780429282591-8

culturally dying town, redefine what a productive worker is or add dignity to the aesthetic traditions of an ethnic minority.

China is renowned for its Great Tradition – its accomplishments in the arts, philosophy, and spirituality. Its cadres manage megacities with steady supplies of water, energy, food, and waste removal. The vast majority of its population has basic literacy. Its capacity for digital innovation makes it the world's leading mobile economy. What value do the social enterprises add to all this? They could be seen as a component of the re-sinification drive of the Xi era. Re-sinification has been added to the productivist ideology and does not detract from the original premise of economic development first. In political terms, re-sinification may be interpreted as communicating a wish for stronger CCP control of the population, for Han dominance over ethnic minorities or neo-nationalism in the global arena. It may also be a stronger accentuation of the social in the productivist premise. If so, this adds strength to the social enterprises' mission's of increasing sociality and civility. However, re-sinification calls for a particular *Chinese* sociality, which adds to the complexity. Particularity is necessary to shape identity and a sense of belonging. The problem for social enterprises is that this requires inclusion and exclusion based on other premises than social needs. Then again, particularism runs contrary to the universalist communist ideology, to the simple premise of communal life – that people need each other, which is a premise in the mission of the social enterprises too. For the social enterprises then, does the direction of social engineering mean that social inclusion and civilised society is limited to people and practices compatible with Chinese culture? Are they partaking in a particularist, nationalist discourse or a universalist, humanist one? Either way, their achievement is to demonstrate that social inclusion and civilised society do not have to wait until social engineering are achieved.

## Digital connectivity and social inclusion

The discussion of the social enterprises has been dotted with references to digital technology. As access to digital technology is a new condition for being social, the have-nots are excluded, so digitalisation both enhances and severs connectivity. In China, however, digitalisation includes and excludes in other ways too.

Digitalisation has changed the Chinese economy radically in the Xi era. Domestically, China has the highest number of mobile Internet users in the world. E-commerce reaches the most remote corners of this vast country. Several Chinese corporations in these industries are among the highest-ranked corporations in the world. These corporations designed and refined their digital platforms in China. Their disruptive technologies have shaped e-commerce, the gaming industry and social media in China. Digital platforms have opened up for economic and political participation on an unprecedented scale and for digital connectivity across the vast continent. Has it also led to better social inclusion?

The three social enterprises have benefitted from digital connectivity in numerous ways. The Institute uses it to maintain markets and ship its products globally. Digital information about DEW appears on the home pages of companies in many other countries. These companies use cyberspace to brand themselves as socially responsible and to spread the word about DEW. The Academy publishes its accounts on a digital platform to provide the Party and its volunteers with easy access to information. However, while digitalisation enhances connectivity, it has also reduced it.

The Chinese government has been quick to adopt digital means to supervise and monitor the population. It has cordoned off Chinese society from global connections through so-called Internet Firewall security that stops unwanted information from leaving or entering the country. This has reduced the social enterprises' ability to communicate digitally with foreign benefactors if the communication touches issues that censors have defined as prohibited. In order to use digital technology to engage in proper dialogue with their stakeholders, the enterprises must keep track of currently allowed topics of conversation and the continuous stream of new sites and groups. This uses precious time that could be spent soliciting funds, competence, moral support, and other resources that foreign benefactors contribute. Thus they are required to disconnect in order to connect.

Digitalisation also diverts social enterprises from their mission, especially the need to be open to the needs and idiosyncrasies of their beneficiaries. When these needs run contrary to what the digital technologies allow, they reduce the social enterprises' ability to meet them where they are. Hence, digitalisation is not a reliable means to communicate the unconditional acceptance of the social worth of the beneficiary that their mission calls for.

Digitalisation excludes and includes simultaneously. The achievement of the social enterprises is that they deal with this contradiction without letting it hinder their social mission.

## Marginalised groups

Marginalisation equals exclusion. By embracing marginalised groups the social enterprises counteract exclusion and make inclusion central. This changes them and the lives of their beneficiaries in the process.

Chinese social enterprises and their beneficiaries are influenced differently by the forces of marginalisation. There is no escape for those who feel they belong in, or are categorised into, groups defined as socially marginal. While this identification gives a sense of community and access to care and resources, it is also a source of exclusion. Social enterprises, on their part, risk being marginalised "by association." Marginalisation is a strong force, even when actively discouraged. A salient example from China is the result of the work-life inclusion policy, whereby corporations are required to hire people with disabilities or pay a fee. The result is that corporations hire people with disabilities and pay them to stay at home.

Marginalisation of social "outliers" is common, not only in China. The poor, handicapped, ill, minorities, and generally anyone who is challenged or too culturally different in some way, is kept out of sight or keeps out of sight, barely tolerated. The understanding of their problems are diverse, ranging from the medical, spiritual, educational, moral and economic. Whatever the explanation, one thing these groups have in common is that they need extra care or help, for a while or permanently. The marginalised also include people who have no family, colleagues, friends or neighbours to help them out, and frequently those who are deemed morally unworthy, socially awkward, permanently damaged, or generally difficult. This is particularly problematic in Chinese society where being social and cultured is so highly valued. Those who do not fit in, whatever the reason, have a weak position from which to make claims on society. They are excluded by definition. How can they then prove their social worth?

What social enterprises do is to provide the marginalised with opportunities to counteract this definition and instead experience their social worth. It may take a long time, after years of disability, or it may happen in the course of days and weeks. At DEW, those who have previous experience with some form of mastery, no matter how mundane, only need basic training to begin to see themselves as proper workers. Others, whether they are pampered or maltreated, need help to redefine who they are first. Not all social enterprises have social missions that explicitly addresses social worth in this manner, but all acknowledge the dignity of the beneficiaries they have chosen to serve.

Although social enterprises work closely with marginalised groups, they must also establish distinctions between their beneficiaries and the enterprise for various purposes. In order to bid for projects, report results, and organise activities. This is required whether marginalised groups start the enterprise or not. People with handicaps have successfully established social organisations of many kinds, as have poor people and the mentally ill. However, every now and then the representatives of social enterprises must exit their protective bubble and operate in accordance with the requirements of mainstream society. While the social enterprise is a start-up, the requirements are even stronger, as the enterprises must prove they are reliable service providers.

Social enterprises associate with and are associated with marginalised groups. Their accomplishment is to make themselves marginal and central, as needs be, and not to be cast away by the forces of marginalisation.

## Public humiliation

Public humiliation and ostracism are common forms of punishment in China. Deviant behaviour and transgressions are by definition unsocial, and so disclosing them for all to see is a means for society to rebalance. Yet, the humiliation marks distinctions and sets people apart. The practice of public humiliation is both social and unsocial at the same time.

In the Xi era, public humiliation and ostracism as forms of reprimand and punishment have become more common. Millions of Party members have lost their membership due to allegations of corruption and fraud in widely publicised cases. The Party has its internal disciplinary institutions, so overstepping is by no means acceptable for members, but to be cast out is worse as that means loss of connections, knowledge and resources, and is decidedly unsocial. The same mechanisms are at work at every level of society. Information about misbehaviour is published on village boards by the authorities. Every person has a dossier, kept updated by locals tasked with maintaining registries over deviant behaviour. The plan for a digital social credit system to monitor people's moral behaviour is a new version of the older system. There is intense social pressure to stay in line. This goes both ways, for many government agencies it is mandatory to have websites where the population may assess their services and leave comments and critique. Everywhere people are humiliated or cast out for not having moral integrity, expressing political opposition, or bending the rules.

Public humiliation can also be practised with exquisite finesse in everyday situations. I saw it at the lunch event when the Beijing "friend" was challenged about being a spy when he brought his mobile phone with him to the washroom. It could have been a warning to the rest of us or it could have been a reminder about hygiene standards. Either way he was visibly embarrassed. I observed numerous other examples of public humiliation, sometimes satirical, sometimes unbendingly judgmental, sometimes with life-threatening consequences, in others merely embarrassing loss of face.

I did not observe such punishing behaviour in the social enterprises' dealings with the beneficiaries, either in face-to-face interaction with them or in conversations about them. It was as if the beneficiaries had invisible protection from further degradation. Social enterprises give a voice to outcasts and defend their dignity and social worth.

## Politics or care?

For social enterprises, political protest against conditions that generate social problems is ethical and unethical at the same time.

Social enterprises are engaged in providing social services to the needy. Some problems are created by government policies, some by corporate strategies. Some problems result from the breaking of rules, some from force majeure. In all of these instances, a social enterprise may choose to protest against the policies, how a crisis is handled, or the rules themselves. That would be an ethical stance. Engaged foreigners often expect oppositional stances from locals. How is it possible to not mobilise, not protest in the face of glaringly visible oppression and injustice? Likewise, it is clearly an ethical stance to report on those whose problems spring from breaking the rules. This upholds the social order and brings problems out in the open. By sharing information, the causes of problems can be identified and better solutions found than anyone can manage on their own. There is also the issue of priority. Why spend time and effort on people who continue to abuse drugs, engage in risky sexual behaviour, or refuse to see the point of the ideology?

The reverse position is that it is not possible to give help without placing the needs of the beneficiary above every other consideration. Social enterprises gain intimate knowledge about the lives and living conditions of their beneficiaries. They learn about embarrassing social conditions, about not being able to read, give a gift, about being abandoned. This enables them to help alleviate social problems. It also provides invaluable information for use in campaigns and political action. However, that would be using the beneficiaries as pawns on the political gaming board. Some social enterprises choose activism but not directly in combination with caregiving.

Life is not logical. Imposing logical stricture on social enterprises in the way I have done above is barely possible. Yet, the explication brings out clearly how they contribute, if not to change, at least to add nuances to the social contract in the domains of the economy, technology, order, law, politics, and ethics. They do this not in a linear, means-end fashion, but by living with the paradoxes, the complexities, yet they manage to grow, by means of continuous balancing between contradictory demands.

## Three lessons

There are many good books about how to start and manage a social enterprise. The early academic pioneers referred to in Chapter 1 are good sources of information. I have no ambition to match this literature. However, it is possible to distil lessons from the social enterprises analysed in the previous chapters. Three lessons, in particular, are relevant. All relate to who the social enterprises are, their organisational identity and their culture.

### *Deciding where to go*

When it comes to deciding where to start an engagement, the keyword is particularity. Careful consideration of the particulars of the place to set up an enterprise is crucial for any business, but social enterprises in China need to take a deeper look at the specific social and cultural context.

China is vast, but also one single polity. Many studies of social enterprises in China have documented the formative power of the general legal framework that includes government policies on social innovation and social work. The legal framework, however, differs between the economic spheres, which are governed by different state bodies and policies. Understanding the differences between the domestic, planned sphere and the international, market sphere is crucial. Even though China has implemented many market mechanisms, the country is not on the verge of turning into a market economy. Far from it. The hegemony of the CCP and the Leninist management culture is not likely to disappear anytime soon. Market mechanisms are used to improve that system, not replace it.

Another source of particularity is the nationality or the ethnicity of the social entrepreneur. The difference between the spheres remains regardless of whether the social entrepreneur is a Chinese national or a foreigner. Many social enterprises have been started in the autonomous ethnic minority regions and areas, which requires careful thought about ethnic positioning. Being a Chinese national in the international sphere is different from being a foreigner and vice versa. Foreigners who want to contribute in the domestic sphere depend on their personal connections with locals but if they only aim to contribute in the international sphere, they do not. Both non-Han Chinese nationals and foreigners have a disadvantage and an advantage in the moral economy. They are freer to innovate because they are not judged by local cultural demands, yet without deep knowledge and understanding of local customs and mores have a harder time following their social mission statement.

The third aspect of particularity is that demand and need for services vary with geographic location, whether in the urban or the rural areas. Such distinctions cut across economic spheres. Needs are larger in the poorer remote areas and here the public social services are less developed, which generates ample opportunities for social enterprises. Resources are scarcer in the remote areas, making the already precarious circumstances that most social enterprises are in, even more difficult.

Finally, the cultural understanding of disability and distress varies between communities, regions and spheres. Where everyone is poor, circumstances that appear as poverty to outsiders, may not be experienced as such. Where disability is interpreted as a moral problem, it is more likely to be hidden away. Where active information campaigning or education has been carried out by other social organisations, local understandings may have changed. Lesson one then is to take all of these issues into consideration when deciding where to start the enterprise.

## *"Barefoot" revolutionaries*

In the area of relevant competence for social enterprises, the keyword is diversity. A social entrepreneur with social work experience had the business idea that launched DEW. DEW has even devised new management positions that include supported employment competence. Many social enterprises employ social workers. This is where the similarities end when it comes to the education and training of people who engage in social enterprises in China. The Academy looked for teachers and got an administrator. The Institute needed embroiderers and got artists and shamans. What social enterprises need are people who known how to do social work, community work, consult, and train. People with professional management experience, who know how to plan, staff, and control operations are also in high demand, and people who can do marketing, negotiate, do accounts, raise funds, source donations – in short, people with a business background. Social enterprises are not the domain of one type of competence but depend on an interdisciplinary approach, on people who are willing to serve as a "jack of all trades," even if they have their training in one specific discipline.

Training and education to become a social entrepreneur is available in China, as in other countries. However, this training is more directed towards the process of starting a social enterprise, how to identify and test a business idea, how to mobilise resources, report on impact – all the managerial skills needed in a well-run, viable operation. The business community has carried its share of the burden of enabling social entrepreneurship and innovation. Not so in many of the other disciplines that could have made a difference: Social work, nursing, teaching, public administration. Neither business nor entrepreneurship is high on their learning agendas. However, many people with professional backgrounds engage in social enterprises so that the required skills or knowledge are available, even if only intermittently from volunteers.

To engage in social enterprises is to accept that no discipline is inherently better or more valuable than another, only that they are different and needed for different purposes. The same goes for the level of competence. Social enterprises do not need people who know everything; they need people who know enough of something to find a practical solution. In the Mao era, lack of health facilities was enormous, especially in the countryside. Those that existed were poorly funded and it was a problem to get enough trained doctors and nurses to settle in remote rural areas. Hence, the "barefoot doctor" scheme was devised. Local farmers, villagers, and practitioners of traditional Chinese medicine got rudimentary medical training in hospitals by qualified doctors. With this training, they were sent back to their villages and provided basic, but much needed healthcare. Higher education was not necessary to be accepted as a practitioner and gender balance was promoted. The barefoot doctors brought modern healthcare to Chinese society. This is why I have called the people in the social enterprises "barefoot" revolutionaries. Without any disrespect for the true revolutionaries in the Party, these "barefoot" change agents go about making ever-so-slight changes to Chinese society. Often with little training, and not for political reasons or with brute force, but with a passion and devotion that are no less ardent than that of proper revolutionaries.

Lesson number two then is that equally important as the consideration of place is the consideration of competence. What kind of professionals are needed, who can be trained, but more importantly, who is devoted enough? Sometimes it is not possible to have both the desired place and the desired people. There is no way to say which of the two to prioritise, only that they must be addressed, either by finding a new place or by training people.

### *The social mission*

Lesson number three is that while exploring where to start and who to mobilise is crucial, this will only really work if there is an explicit, communicable, and communicated social mission. A social mission is simply the expression of a cause or an end goal that will benefit society. The job of a social mission is to be a symbol around which different stakeholders can find meaning. They may not all find the same meaning even, but enough to create a sense of community. The social mission will be used repeatedly. It needs to be resilient, versatile, and concrete, at least to inspire practical action. It describes the (utopian) end goal and therefore gives direction. It gives meaning and therefore understanding. It is a measuring rod and a means to prioritise. Not a small job for a few simple words.

There are several reasons why the social mission is so crucial. First, there are more social problems than any single social enterprise can possibly deal with. It also usually takes a long time and effort on many fronts to achieve lasting results. Therefore, honing in on one particular issue, and sticking with it, is key for establishing a viable enterprise.

A social mission sometimes arrives as a spark of inspiration during a conversation, a dream or a meditation. In the myths of the aid industry, histories of such revelations are common. An oft-cited example is the expression "reverence for life," which inspired the work of the multitalented Swiss doctor and missionary Albert Schweitzer in Africa. It is said to have come to him during a train ride. Whatever the background for the initiative, divine inspiration or a chance meeting, grasping the expression of a mission, testing it, exploring what it actually means and can mean, takes time. That is time well spent, especially if the quest for a particular meaning for a particular enterprise engages its stakeholders.

The social mission is extra important in China because it is a way to connect with the Party, the dominant hegemony comprising 80 million people and innumerable communiques and policy statements. As the experiences of the Institute exemplified, standing up to CCP demands is possible if backed by arguments grounded in a culturally legitimate reason for being. It is also a way to keep the enterprise on course in meeting the demands of other influential stakeholders, including idealistic volunteers and members.

## Conclusion

The aim of this book was to dig into China's social discourse. In the introduction, I asked if China is on the road to dictatorship or predatory competition. It could go both ways. The country certainly has experienced much of both, with 30 years of communist rule and 40 years of market reform. This was written before the Covid-19 pandemic hit the globe in 2020, but that has not pushed the country into either of those directions. China stands strong in the wave of digitalisation, marketisation, globalisation, and a pandemic on top of that. Judging from the efforts of social enterprises, and those who engage with them, the social entrepreneurs contribute to craft a new China, with considerable care and respect for the social contract that binds state and society.

# Index

Printed in the United States
by Baker & Taylor Publisher Services